HUNTED

A true story of survival

HUNTED

A true story of survival

David Fletcher

CARROLL & GRAF PUBLISHERS
New York

Carroll & Graf Publishers
An imprint of Avalon Publishing Group, Inc.
161 William Street
New York
NY 10038 2607
www.carrollandgraf.com

First published in the UK by Constable,
an imprint of Constable & Robinson Ltd 2002

First Carroll & Graf edition 2002

ISBN 0-7867-0998-7

Printed and bound in the EU

Library of Congress Cataloging-in-Publication Data is available on file.

To my wonderful children
Delia Anne
Sarah Jane
Callum
Dana

Contents

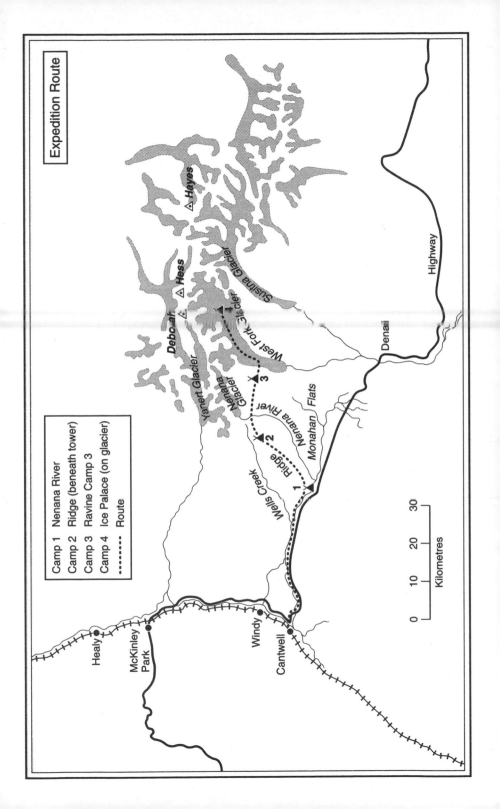

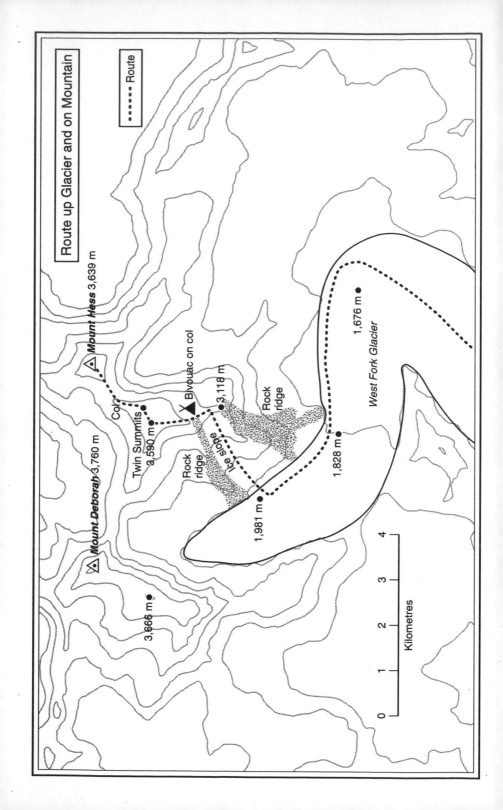

Route up Glacier and on Mountain

...... Route

Mount Hess 3,639 m

Mount Deborah 3,760 m

3,666 m

Twin Summits 3,590 m

Col

Bivouac on col

3,118 m

Rock ridge

Ice slope

Rock ridge

1,981 m

1,828 m

1,676 m

West Fork Glacier

0 1 2 3 4

Kilometres

Author's Note

The events that are described in this book took place over a decade ago but still live with me as if they had occurred last month. Afterwards I was in shock. My hair went white overnight – I didn't know that really happens but it does – and my voice almost disappeared. I could no more have rushed off to sell my story than I could have turned round and returned to the summit of Mount Hess.

Over the intervening years I made various attempts to get the facts down on paper but only last year did I feel sufficiently distanced to be able to get to the end of my story. When I did so I found I still had total recall of the journey into the mountains, my ascent of Mount Hess and all my nightmare encounters with the bear. I clearly remember descending the glacier on day nine. From then on days and nights merged, I was severely traumatized by the ferocity of the bear attacks, especially at the end, and realize there are some days unaccounted for in the final crossing of the wilderness which passed in a blur of pain and sorrow. Apart from that, this is a true account of one man taking on the Alaskan wilderness – and its inhabitants.

David Fletcher
Kingston-upon-Hull, 2002

Chapter 1

The Challenge

"Anything to declare?" asks the US Customs official in the friendly-suspicious tone of voice which goes with the job. I've arrived at Anchorage through portentiously dramatic skies in May, 1980.

"Nothing to declare!" I reply.

"Where was it last time?" he asks, eying the earlier Alaskan stamps in my passport, the last one dated the year before. "McKinley?"

"Yes. I'm hoping to climb Mount Hess this time!"

He makes a face of surprise but all he says is, "Good luck!" as he brings down the Anchorage stamp for the fourth time on a fresh page.

My choice of Mount Hess has not been arrived at quickly and involved a number of sessions in the Kingston-upon-Hull public library as I filled out a large notebook with the more important and difficult peaks of Alaska. One by one I began to cross them off the list. The Coast Ranges were too wet and windy. The Brooks Range in the far north was not high enough for my liking. This left the Alaska Range. The ease of access from the railroad made these mountains an ideal choice. The rail track cuts through them on its way from Anchorage to Fairbanks. To the east of the railroad stands the beautiful Hayes group of mountains, isolated, rarely visited, but savagely beautiful. To the west of the track the Denali National Park encompasses most of the highest peaks in the area, including Denali itself, the highest summit in North America, formerly known as Mount McKinley, which I'd attempted on my last trip.

The popularity of the National Park and the inevitable accompanying regulations ruled that area out for me. Time to explore the other side of the tracks. So it was to be the Hayes group, with a choice of the three main peaks, Mount Deborah, Mount Hess and Mount Hayes. I chose to climb the central peak, Mount Hess (3639m), because it is the least talked about, visited and documented of the three. There is also good access to the mountain from the Denali Highway to the south, but this is for strong walkers only through some real and wonderful wilderness country.

I push through the Arrivals door into the open air and there is John, a climbing friend of long standing who has appointed himself my support team. He is leaning smiling, arms folded, against the side of his pick-up truck with the largest pair of snowshoes I've ever seen propped in the back. (These ancient objects are about to be on loan to me.)

"Where to, David?"

There's no need for me to think long and hard about that question. The answer is simple. "Anywhere that serves food."

Soon John and I are joined by other friends to talk climbing as we feast on piled platefuls of chicken drumsticks, eggs, beans and chips, not the usual spindly little French fries normally served up in Europe either, but great big Alaskan chips, solid, absolutely dependable man-sized chips and lots and lots of bright red tomato sauce. I even come up for seconds, as if my body is already stoking itself up for what lies ahead.

Afterwards John parks his pick-up outside my hotel and we unfold the huge map of Alaska and spread it on our knees to study by the glow of the overhead cab light. It's time to make some important decisions.

I explain that I plan to take the train next morning as far as Cantwell, walk east along the Denali Highway towards Wells Creek, then strike off north into the wilderness, aiming for the side of the West Fork Glacier which should lead me to the foot of Mount Hess.

Put like that it sounds pretty straightforward but I can see John has doubts about the wisdom of what I'm planning to do solo and unsupported. He tries half-heartedly to persuade me to attempt something less demanding, or at least to accept a food drop by air. I tell him I'll have enough food for ten days and then can live off the land. We both know that last bit's a joke because where I plan to be at the end of ten days there will be nothing. So the joke falls flat. When John sees arguing is a lost cause, he agrees to be on the highway with his truck looking out for me ten days from now.

"That's plenty of time for you to get in, get up the mountain, and out again." He hesitates. "So at what point should I give up waiting for you and call out the rescue services?"

There is a silence as I stare blankly out through the windscreen into space. It's warm inside the cab, very warm, and I wipe the sweat from my forehead. John winds down his window. I don't know what to answer.

"Well, whatever you decide, if I do have to come out and look for you, I'll bring an aircraft in over the Main West Fork Glacier first. That's bound to be one of your big risk areas."

We agree on a full three weeks before he does this and I make him promise not to jump the gun.

That night sleep takes me off into a wonderful Alaskan dreamland, full of pure white polar bear fur, a curious moose, a rosy red fox, a playful beaver, a fabulously rich mink, a cautious lynx, powerful grizzly bears and flat-footed snow-shoe hares. Delicious edible berries will soon be ripening in the summer sun. They will melt in the mouth, blueberries, cranberries, cloud berries, so light airy and fluffy . . .

So ignorant. So tired.

It's a relief to leave the confines of the train and step down into the crisp air of the Alaskan interior. Freedom surrounds me now. The damp woods beckon. A clear absence of time is everywhere. The haunting cry of the timber wolf cannot be far away.

There are no station buildings at Cantwell, just a railroad track, a pile of logs, and a dog, tail wagging, as it waits for its owner.

The huge wooden doors of the baggage car are already open and the guard hands down my luggage – struggling under its weight. "What have we here?"

"Just climbing equipment," I reply.

The words, "Good Luck!" drift back from the guard, as the train pulls away from the station, slowly at first, until gradually gaining speed for its long journey on to Fairbanks. Silence descends on the station, the dog, realizing I'm not for him, lies down, head resting on its paws in the snow, blinking, watching and waiting for its owner.

I pick up my rucksack, it's time to go. After hours of cramped inactivity on the train, I'm now stiff and sore, but bursting full of energy. My boots crunch in the gravel of the side road leading up to the junction with the Denali Highway. Numerous squirrels seem quite unconcerned at my passing. They just pause for a moment to look up, then carry on doing whatever it was that they were doing in the first place.

I'm now faced with the dreary prospect of walking thirty odd kilometres along the Denali Highway before I can step off into the wilderness. But the thought of all that untouched forest waiting for me pushes me onwards. I concentrate on placing my boots on the ground, in the most energy-saving manner possible.

Heels high up onto the sharp stones. Trying to keep the rigid soles of my climbing boots level at all times. Zigzagging where possible. Never taking a slope head on. Uphill, downhill.

Then, suddenly, I'm sure I can hear a vehicle behind me. It's a truck.

"You want a lift?"

The driver opens the door for me. Self-sufficiency begins further on, I tell myself. The driver looks surprised at seeing someone out alone on the highway.

"Where you from?"

"Cantwell," I reply.

"That's some walk you've just done! And where you headed for? You do know there's nothing out here, no communities, no settlements . . ."

I try to explain my climbing plans and he agrees to drop me off at Wells Creek. We set off in a loud screech of gravel and spinning tyres, my pack bouncing around in the back of the truck. It's all I can do to hang on to my seat for dear life, a little worried that I may end up back out on the road again.

The driver is happy to let me do most of the talking. But when I raise the subject of fishing, he takes over. He is a fisherman through and through. He talks of rivers, lakes, rod and line with all the passion and enthusiasm that I feel for climbing. His eyes light up when I mention that I've always wanted to try my hand at fishing for salmon. I hope to do this on the approach to the mountain.

"But watch out for the bears!" he warns.

"Bears?" I ask.

I can feel the sense of fun draining out of one of my long cherished dreams. Perhaps the idea of fishing isn't such a good one after all.

We continue to talk about all things Alaskan, passing over numerous small bridges spanning crystal clear mountain streams, bubbling and dancing down, looking for the shortest route to the sea.

I must be in the Wells Creek area by now, although, to be absolutely truthful, I've been far too busy talking to the driver to be sure of my position. But it doesn't really matter. The way towards the Nenana Glacier, my first check-point on my journey across the wilderness, is obvious. It's there in amongst those towering white peaks on the northern horizon.

The driver pulls over to the side of the road, although still questioning the soundness of my decision.

"What? Here? In the middle of nowhere?"

There's a look of genuine concern on his face, now. If my trip had been for anything else, for hunting, for fishing, or even, for gold prospecting, all would have been understandable.

"Climbing?" he said, "You're crazy. You got no rifle with you? Better take some more of these!" Already he has given me the majority of his reindeer steak sandwiches while we were chatting. I'm overcome by his generosity. To this day I don't know the name of that man.

An exceptionally fine shower of snow dust is thrown

up by the rear wheels of his truck as he drives his lonely way on to Paxson. There, according to his own estimation, the most perfect fishing awaits him, at Summit Lake.

If I had any doubts about this trip, now would be as good a time as any to exercise them. I could still turn around and get back to Cantwell. But I know I'll accomplish my expedition as planned – within my own given set of rules.

1 The first rule to follow is my own long and difficult approach route into the mountains. There are easier and more direct ways to reach Mount Hess on foot, but I prefer the unique challenge of my way.
2 I must travel alone.
3 I will carry no weapons of any kind.
4 I must carry everything needed on my own back, there are no air drops for me here.
5 I must walk in and out unaided, except, of course, in an emergency.
6 I must achieve my climb at its purest with no reconnaissance of my route up the mountain. (I have not even looked at a photograph of Mount Hess.)

All this will not be easy, but if I had wanted an easy time of it, I would have returned to the European Alps, soft bunk beds, cable cars, guidebooks and all.

Instead of feeling intimidated, I suddenly feel full of

enthusiasm, ready for the journey ahead. I look forward to the challenges my expedition will bring, and the first of these is finding a good camping spot to spend the night. The Nenana River can't be that far from here. The other side of the river would be an ideal place to erect a tent. By crossing the river, I'd have all night to dry my clothing out.

The moment I step off the highway, I'm onto wet snow, not total cover, just the occasional damp patch, here and there. The water continues to squelch up around my boots as I approach the Nenana River. One minute I'm in the woods, the next I'm surrounded by the smell, then the sound of running water. My boot prints press hard into the central island sandbar of the river.

Having found my ideal campsite at my first attempt, and erected my tent, I'm far too tired to do anything else. Instead I lie eating my remaining reindeer steak sandwiches, deep inside my sleeping bag, looking up at the bright red orange fabric of my inner tent. Nothing else seems to matter. If only the weather could remain like this, with beautiful, all red, orange and pink sunsets, and no storms at all. But I doubt it. Still, I can hope.

I've allowed myself two whole days in which to cross the wilderness. By then I should be well and truly established on the ice of the Main West Fork Glacier, surrounded by mountains I have not yet seen and about which I can only dream.

Chapter 2

The Cub

After packing my equipment away, along with ten days' supply of food, I set off full of enthusiasm for the snout of the narrow Nenana Glacier some twenty-five kilometres away. The object of first heading for this prominent feature is that it represents a clear check-point on my journey across an otherwise featureless wilderness.

Tiny droplets of water cling to my hair and clothing as I walk beneath the forest canopy. It's a magical walk in a peaceful world, full of small squirrel movements, which can just be seen out of the corner of my eye, tiny water-filled rivulets underfoot, and face-brushing spiders' webs all around me. These eventually come to an end, after several hours' pleasant walking, swallowed up in the mist of a more open terrain of alternating cottonwood clumps and moist tundra meadows.

The foothills stretch out before me, like a huge arrow pointing the way into the high mountains, making it very difficult for me to get lost. Once the Nenana

Glacier comes into view, sometime late this evening or early tomorrow morning, I'll alter course over to the east, heading out towards my big glacier destination at West Fork.

The snow becomes more widespread now, weighing down the lighter cottonwood branches on the ridges but leaving the hollows in a deep shadowy layer. I fasten my snowshoes onto my boots and begin to float over the surface, instead of sinking down into it at every step. Not even the dense cottonwood tangles can stop me now.

The wind gradually begins to clear the mist. Perhaps if I wait up here on the west side of the ridge until it clears up, I'll be able to see the view that has been hidden from me for so long.

I settle down on a convenient rock and crunch hungrily into a bar of chocolate. When my crunching stops the silence starts to become apparent. I haven't noticed this silence before. There's just the faint whisper of the wind and the pleasant sound of water running deep underground. But there's not a single sound, from any animal to be heard anywhere. When I come to think of all the animal tracks that I've passed on the way up here, surely the creatures that made them must still be around, and be making some kind of noise? But there's nothing to be heard anywhere.

The mist closes in once more. There's just the odd patch of countryside to be peeped at here and there as it thins out a little. Perhaps if I wait up here a little while longer . . .

I've got ten small oranges packed away inside my rucksack, one for each of the ten days that I'll be away. I think I'll eat one now.

Halfway through peeling my orange, however, I freeze, when I spot a tiny movement below me on the floor of the valley.

I'm sure I saw something move down there in the mist in amongst the trees in the bottom of the valley. A small forward movement. A dark black shape, perhaps, creeping through the woods. What kind of animal would be doing that at this time in the morning? It could be a black sheep, although, all the creatures of that species around here, Dall sheep, I think, are white in colour, aren't they? And sheep don't go creeping through the woods at this time in the morning? Do they? The movement that I saw was most probably a goat. I sit back down to finish off peeling my orange, (I'm not really interested in goats).

The mist lingers on and on and I continue to wait it out up here on the side of the ridge. I could do with a rest anyway, my rucksack's far too heavy. There's still the most awful deathly silence permeating the mist. I'll be glad when it has finally cleared up and I've moved on.

I seem to have been staring down at this hole in the ground directly in front of me for some time now. It looks very similar to several more I've passed tunnelled into the hillside on the way up here. In fact there are holes everywhere. It's as if a whole army of moles has been at work on the slopes leading up from the very bottom of the valley to a point high on this ridge. If it isn't the work of moles, what kind of creature could have possibly caused all this upheaval? A gopher? A goat? Yet, I know the truth. Only a bear could have made these holes, tunnelling into the ground with its two huge front paws, in the hope of finding something to eat. A succulent ground squirrel perhaps or some tasty green roots. In fact anything edible until a more substantial meal can be hunted down and killed. What an enormous appetite this bear must have if the large number of holes in the area are anything to go by. Perhaps it's time I altered my route. I've got to take a line that will keep me as high above the floor of the valley as possible. This will reduce the possibility of an encounter with a bear to a minimum. I quickly shoulder my rucksack and set off, climbing directly up the west side of the ridge. Only this time I'm moving a little faster. I've got a real incentive to move now. I'm spurred on by fear.

I've always found it an effort, especially when carrying a heavy rucksack, to climb directly up a steep snow slope. Today is no exception. The slightest irregular movement I make, causes the sack to swing over to one side and threaten to throw me off balance. I persevere until stopped by a short wall of rock. But I'm high enough above my original traverse line now to feel safe. I pause to regain my breath. The valley floor does seem a long way below me now.

I begin to traverse along the side of the ridge, just a

short distance below the crest, happy and contented for the moment that height is safety, and that I'm well out of reach of any bears that might be around.

The Nenana Glacier can't be that far ahead of me now, perhaps some ten hours away from here at the most, at the end of this ridge.

Once I find the snout of the Nenana Glacier, and I can clearly identify this prominent feature on the ground, which should be sometime this evening or early tomorrow morning, I'll turn away to the east, contouring the head of Monahan Flats, a low swampy area draining the Hayes group to the north of the Denali Highway, and head directly for the side of the Main West Fork Glacier. At least that's the theory. No one has ever tried to reach the side of this huge glacier from a starting point in the Wells Creek area before. But this is the unique challenge I've been seeking. This is the adventure I crave.

It's a pity that I can't see the mountains I'm headed for now, Mount Hess in particular. The trouble is I'm on the wrong side of the ridge. But I can clearly see the valley floor below me now. Patches of stunted spruce trees edge the highway and river systems at all the lowest levels. Cottongrass and sedges can be seen growing higher still. While all around me, a mass of white flowered dryas are forcing their way out from beneath all the rocks not covered in snow. It's still too early in the season for them to be in full bloom yet. However, the odd bud does peek out from beneath the snow, as I continue on with my journey.

The mist suddenly closes in once more with a vengeance. I begin to probe my way blindly forward. I've got no choice in the matter, if I'm to make any progress. I continue to thrust the shaft of my ice-axe into the ground in front of me, until stopped by a narrow ravine, cutting from top to bottom of the slope.

Negotiating this great gash in the hillside is going to slow me down still further. I've got no option but to lose all the height that I've just gained over these last few hours in order to get around this obstacle. Being stopped by a stream cutting its way down the hillside is a calculated risk that any climber takes when contouring a slope. There's only one way around this type of problem. I've got to climb down into the ravine itself. I can't possibly climb around the head of this obstacle, there's a waterfall blocking the way. Then I've got to follow the ravine all the way down into the bottom of the valley to where I hope it will peter out, then reascend the slope on the other side to regain my previous high point.

I prepare to abseil into the ravine. Like a spider on a warm new-spun silken thread, I spiral down into the mist caused by the water thrown out past the overhanging rock, and into the rising crescendo of noise from the sheer weight of the water jostling the loose boulders about on the floor of the ravine. My boots hit the gravel bank running alongside the stream with a loud crunch. I'm glad to be down at last.

The ravine is narrow, surprisingly so, there's just enough room for a small stream between the two huge walls and a small walkway of boulders on either side.

I've been toying with the idea of climbing the far wall of the ravine in order to avoid a time-consuming detour, but I can see that any attempt to do this is out of the question. Every possible ledge, foothold and handhold, is covered in a thick green slime of mosses and lichens that thrive in this water-laden atmosphere. So I set off carefully along the narrow walkway of rocks bordering the right-hand side of the stream. I feel happy for the moment to be plodding my way slowly down-hill, until my boulder-hopping footpath comes to an abrupt stop and I'm forced tight up against the right-hand wall. Where on earth can I put my feet now? I don't want to get them wet if I can help it. I definitely don't want to get my clothing soaked. I'm left high and dry on top of a rock, water swirling all around me. I must get across to the other side of the stream if I'm to carry on with my journey down the ravine. It looks like I'm going to have to jump across it. (The water at this point is far too deep for me to wade through.) The trouble here is that all the rocks on the far bank of the stream look very icy to me. I can see what's going to happen next, but I have no choice. I jump the stream in one great bounding leap with my boots easily clearing the top of the highest surge of water beneath me. I slip on the far bank, I half expected that I would, and stagger slowly backwards into the snow, sitting down somewhat unceremoniously, surrendering to the inevi-table. But getting my clothing covered in snow is far better than getting a good soaking. I can't afford to get my feet or my clothing wet in the icy cold temperatures down here in the bottom of the ravine.

The snow seems to have got in everywhere. As I brush the last remaining snowflakes from my clothing, I watch them flutter slowly to the ground, landing inside several large hollows that mark the snow's otherwise virgin surface. But surely these are not the normal water-melting hollows seen around the banks of a fast flowing stream. These are bear tracks! I can clearly see the claw marks at the front of each wide depression. The shock to my system is enormous. The awful truth dawns on me, that if the bear that made those tracks comes back, I'll be in for a head-on encounter as it climbs up the ravine.

The sooner I get out of here the better.

I know that there are bears in Alaska, somewhere in the region of fifty thousand brown bears at the last count. I know it is wise to give one a warning of your approach, so that it can move out of your way. At least that's the theory – make a noise, any noise, by blowing a whistle, by ringing a bell, or by rattling a stone in an empty tin can. A bear caught by surprise will attack, thinking it is being threatened. But it's the giant grizzly bear that I fear the most, and the one that I must avoid at all costs. I can only hope that one of those monstrous creatures is not waiting for me downstream.

One might think that if I'd brought a high-powered rifle with me I'd be more than a match for a bear. For all my Royal Marine training this is not so. To stand your ground and fire at a creature that can kill you is a totally different proposition to firing at a fixed target. I was taking a calculated risk here. I was balancing off the weight of a rifle and ammunition against the unlikely event of meeting a bear.

My own tracks in the snow now seem to be matching the bear's precisely. I continue to step in the best places only to find that the huge front and rear paws have been there before me. This is one creature that certainly knows how to travel over the ground by the easiest route, but then it would, this is its home territory.

I begin to feel very nervous indeed.

I must remain calm at all costs. Yet it's so hard to stay composed when facing such an obvious threat. I find myself tightening my grip on my ice-hammer which I am holding high in front of my face to protect myself from the profusion of sharp pointed branches sticking out of the fissures in the wall of the ravine. Surely I could put my ice-hammer to better use? I could use it to defend myself against a bear. But I must be mad to think that I could do that against an adult male bear when a man with a high-powered rifle would be hard pushed to stop one. I'd have to go for a shoulder shot first, to stop it from charging forward, then shoot to kill. But I must be out of my mind! I haven't got a rifle with me. I've got no firearms of any kind with me. I've got no choice now but to get the hell out of here.

The time seems to pass slowly. There's plenty of time for me to criss-cross the stream a dozen more times.

Time for me to avoid countless more sharp branches. There's even time for a slip or two on the icy rocks beneath my feet. But most important of all, there's time for the walls of the ravine to decrease in size as I approach the bottom of the valley. I'm at last able to climb out. Just a few straight forward moves are all that's needed to get me up the scree slope forming the right-hand wall of the ravine. I feel an enormous sense of relief. I can breathe once more. I can move about freely in any direction that I choose. I'm out into a more open rugged countryside full of brush-lined gullies, hills and hollows, and ready to resume my journey back up to my previous high point just below the crest of the ridge itself on the other side of the ravine.

After a bit there are far too many bushes around the edges of a clearing for my liking. I can't see where I'm going at all now. I can't afford to get lost at this critical juncture, but I should be able to get a far better view of the route ahead of me if I stand up on top of this old tree stump. I'm still a little uncertain about the best way forward. I could always start climbing more in towards the very edge of the high ravine wall itself. From my stump I continue to study the slope above me, in greater detail this time, peering up through what little gaps there are in the mist, with my ice-hammer held tightly in my right hand. The idea of climbing as close to the edge of the ravine wall appears to be my best bet. The snow looks less deep and less liable to avalanche.

What the bloody hell was that?

I quickly spin around to the sound of a high-pitched

screaming noise coming from somewhere behind me. But there's nothing to be seen . . . behind me . . . around me. There's still nothing to be seen but bushes and trees and rocks.

When a dark black shape comes running straight towards me, I react almost instinctively, with my ice-hammer still held tightly in my right hand. I raise it high above my head. A split second later several kilograms of razor sharp steel go slicing through the air towards the dark black shape. The moment my ice-hammer leaves my hand and speeds on its way towards the target I realize that I have made the most dreadful mistake imaginable.

I swear to God I meant no harm! I truly swear!

I acted purely out of a sense of self-preservation. In my mind's eye there was this huge bear running towards me, threatening my very existence. I never realized it was only an innocent bear cub. I watch horrified as my ice-hammer strikes the cub full in the face. Fur explodes. It splatters out in all directions, floating high in the ominously still air of the clearing. I can't believe what I have just done. I lift my hands to my face, looking on in absolute utter horror!

The little bear screams out loud. It's a terrible high-pitched scream that seems to go on forever. I watch horrified as it staggers forward towards what must be the entrance to its den, making its way in the direction of the only home it has ever known. And there the little bear remains swaying gently back and forth on its two tiny rear legs in the entrance to the den. There's a long pause before the cub finally falls face down into the blackness of the cave.

Tears form in my eyes as I step forward to pick up my ice-hammer, tears for a wrong that can never be undone. I can truly say that I have never before harmed any creature out here in the wilderness, except under the strictest rules of survival, never for fun, and never intentionally. If only I had blown the whistle that hangs permanently around my neck. The noise would have warned the cub of my approach. It would then have had time to hide away inside the cave. The truth of the matter is that I did think of blowing it, but I was afraid that the noise might attract a bear to me instead of scaring it away. It's all too easy to make judgements after an event. My tears fall into the blood red snow at my feet. It doesn't matter that what happened here was an accident. It doesn't matter how many times I tell the wilderness *I swear to God I meant no harm*. What has happened has taken place, and can never be undone.

My heart pounds in my chest as I vainly try to pretend that the cub was black in colour. Black bears are very timid. They rarely attack human beings. But I can't escape the awful truth. It lies in the snow at my feet, tiny tufts of dark brown hair. Even the cave entrance betrays by its very size the formidable bulk of its owner. Where is the owner of the cave now? One thing's for sure, there's no way that I'm going to stay around here to find out the answer to that question.

On my first trip to Alaska a friend and hunter warned me that a grizzly bear with young cubs under her protection will rarely stray far from her young, preferring to keep them within easy calling range. A bear with cubs knows no fear, and can easily outrun the fastest man. These chilling words come flooding back to me now. My friend's parting advice had been, "Don't you ever underestimate the intelligence of a grizzly bear. They are mean, they are natural killers, but above all, they can think!"

A deathly silence now hangs over the clearing. I must get the hell out of here and fast. I begin to make the long climb back up to my previous high point, just below the crest of the ridge. I must get closer in towards the edge of the ravine wall but above all, I must get as high above the valley floor as possible before the bear finds out what I have done to its cub and starts to come after me.

I try to become invisible against the drifting snow, to no avail. I must be visible the length and breadth of the valley up here. There is nowhere to hide when moving up a plain snow slope outlined against the sky. I bet I can be seen, by someone using a pair of powerful binoculars, from as far away as the cottonwoods along the banks of the Nenana River. I dare not turn around to see if there's a bear following me. It's as if my not seeing will somehow protect me. All my senses scream out at me to run. But all my survival and climbing experience says slow down. I must slow down. I must not slip. Whatever I do I must not lose my balance on such a steep ice slope. I must not draw any undue attention to myself.

I half expect a bear to come creeping up behind me at any moment now. But nothing out of the ordinary is happening up here. There are no sounds coming from anywhere back along my trail either. There are just the normal scraping noises from the front-points on my crampons as they spike alternately into the snow slope in front of me.

I don't feel in any way relieved when I first climb up, then over a small snow ridge. I may be out of sight of any bear following me, but I know full well that it does not track its quarry by sight alone. Bears are short-sighted so mainly use their sense of smell. I must take no chances. I must assume the worst. Now that I'm out of sight of any bear following me, I must fly like the wind up this steep snow slope to the relative safety of the high ground above.

A whole series of icy rocks sticking up from beneath the snow try their level best to slow me down, but my determination is far too strong today and I continue to make excellent progress up through swirls of mist. The mist is a mixed blessing. Although, it is serving to slow me down, it will help to hide me from any bear that is following me. There's only the smallest circle of high-angled snow to be seen in front of me now in the beam of white light radiating down from my headtorch attached to the front of my climbing helmet.

I can only hope that the bear, when it eventually returns, will stay with its dying cub. This will give me the time I need to put more distance between us. I should be safely out of its reach once I'm on the ridge proper. Perhaps the cub will recover? I truly hope that it does. But what of the cub's mother? Perhaps the great bear has already been killed at the hand of some hunter? That would explain why it hasn't caught up with me yet. I'm grasping at straws here. The obvious scenario is that the bear is staying with its dying cub until the end, when it will be carried off to be buried in a shallow grave, clawed out of the deep frozen Alaskan earth. Stories like this have been handed down by the Inuit, from father to son, from time immemorial. From the times when the great bears ruled the land, un challenged, fearing no one, absolute kings, in their icy kingdom. I believe such stories and I have a terrible feeling, deep in the back of my mind, that something dreadful is about to happen to me. It's best then not to waste a single precious moment in making my escape, for there are some stories and some questions that are best left unanswered.

It is here that I receive my second shock of the day. There is this line high above Alaska that seems to divide the bone-shattering freezing cold weather conditions above from the tolerably cold conditions below. This temperature gradient is the most dramatic I've experienced anywhere. It becomes so very cold and icy now, as I pass through this invisible line, but there's no way that I dare stop to put on more clothing, with this terrible nagging fear about what is following me driving me higher.

The ridge creeps up on me almost unnoticed. It suddenly appears in front of me like some wonderful vision from out of the clouds to give me all the energy that I need to climb up the last few tiring pitches. I finally crest the most beautiful snow ridge that I have ever seen.

I can go no higher.

I turn around to look back down my trail. There's no sign of any bear. My trail, zigzagging steeply up the snow slope below me, is completely empty of all life. I think that I'd have died of fright if I'd seen a bear moving around down there. There's only the wind to be heard now, driving the snow before it, trying its level best to fill my trail in, and the all-pervading cold around me. Up here the wind blows wild and free. There is no shelter. A violent shiver shakes me, as I rush to put on more clothing, previously discarded in the warm confines of the ravine. I desperately need my woollen jumpers now. Then I slide my red down jacket over the top and pull the hood forward over my climbing helmet, covering most of my face as well. Now that I'm smothered in luxury, I set off along the ridge looking for a safe place to spend the night.

There are times of walking delicately along the very crest of the ridge with a huge drop on either side of me, and times of walking flat out, in sudden bursts of unexpected energy, and moments best forgotten, of slipping and sliding. But I make good progress, balancing, for most of the time, along the point of the ridge itself, until stopped by a small gap. What a pleasant surprise, instead of meeting more serious obstacles, an almost level ridge greets me, curving gently around to the left.

I continue to stroll along, munching a bar of chocolate. There are eight squares on this particular bar. After the initial bite, I let each one melt in my mouth, as slowly as I possibly can. I must remember to make all the pieces on my bars of chocolate last as long as these eight squares.

A strange noise begins to drift up from somewhere within the confines of the bottom of the valley. I remain quite still, standing in perfect balance on the crest of the ridge, wondering what kind of creature could be making all this noise. If there were some recognizable sounds in amongst all this commotion I could go happily on my way, but curiosity keeps me pausing, and the answer's not long in coming.

The noise begins to sound like a bear rampaging through the undergrowth destroying all before it. The roaring noises continue to grow in intensity. Then, suddenly, a very definite splintering of green timber rends the cold night air. I cover my ears in a desperate attempt to blot it out. But the calamitous sound of timber crashing to the ground still manages to get through. I realize now that the cub must be dead, and that I'm listening to the full fury of the mother.

I begin to move like a bat out of hell now. I'm still looking for a safe place to spend the night. I sweep all before me until coming up against the first of three tall rock towers which obstruct all further progress along the ridge. But I'm in no mood to be stopped by any obstacle now, no matter how difficult. Especially when a bear may be following me. I traverse around the left-hand side of the first tower. Then I climb back up onto the crest, with my crampons biting hard into the long curving sweep of the ridge, leading up to the base of the second tower. I'm never going to be able to climb around the sides of this obstacle, not without getting into some real climbing difficulties. Instead, I climb it direct, straight up the wall confronting me, then down the opposite side. I soon reach the base of the third and final rock tower. Here a perfect bivouac site greets me. Even more important is the fact that the ice drops away steeply on either side.

No bear will be able to reach me up here.

A deep hollow has formed between the base of the tower and a high bank of snow surrounding it. My tent should easily fit inside this gap, with the snow bank offering me a high degree of protection from the wind. It's going to be a lot warmer sleeping in a tent out of the wind. It's hard to contain my delight at finding such a perfect bivouac site.

I set to work levelling the floor of the hollow using the sharp blade of my snow-shovel to great effect. There's nothing worse than sleeping on an uneven sloping surface. Then I use my heavy climbing boots to stamp the snow down, compacting it still further. I quickly erect my tent inside the hollow. Then I spread my groundsheet, karrimat and sleeping bag inside my tent. This triple combination of materials should help to protect me from the vicious cold that will strike up from below during the night. There's just my evening meal to cook now, and one very important last task to perform before I go to sleep, one that if successful will send me off to sleep feeling a great deal safer.

The rock tower, now completely dominating the area of my bivouac site, appears far more formidable to climb than I suspect it really is.

My first moves up the wall of the tower are very cautious indeed. I'm just testing its defences. Then a whole series of big handholds appears, the sort climbers call jugs, standing proud of the rock. I fit my hands neatly around each one in turn and am soon standing up on top of the tower, after mantelshelfing over the well defined edge. An ice-wrinkled but level snowy platform greets me. I feel greatly relieved that my route went so well. But there's a serious motive to this climb. I remove my rope from around my shoulders, then loop it around the complete column of rock, before abseiling back down the side of the tower to land directly opposite the front opening to my tent. My rope now hangs straight down the wall and into the area of my bivouac site. The spare coils will come in useful later on tonight as a pillow. The question still remains: will my elaborate escape route work? I practise climbing in and out of my sleeping bag, then climbing, hand over hand, up my rope, to the safest place around, the top of the tower.

Bears do not necessarily go to sleep at night, a preferred period of activity being the twilight hours. However they will roam in search of prey at any time of the day or night. I've not the slightest intention of becoming the victim of a bear or any other creature out here in the wilderness. I'll just have to be very careful and take similar precautions in all my movements from now on.

It's not long before all three rows of tiny gas jets are flickering on top of my stove. They gradually begin to mesmerize me. I could lie here, wrapped up, safe and warm, inside my tent, all night long, watching them. However, the snow inside my pan has melted and is boiling. Time to tip in the soup powder and soon I am savouring each spicy hot spoonful of meat and veg straight out of the pan. I'm feeling warm all over now, and begin to feel very tired. I could drift off to sleep now and not wake up till morning. Perhaps I'll go to sleep right this minute and not leave the warmth of my tent. But I've got to leave it sooner or later. Fear is going to drive me back outside into the night. I still feel confident that the bear cannot reach me up here. But I could be wrong. The bear might just be able to claw its way up the steep wall of ice below my bivouac site.

I continue to listen, with my head poked out of the warm tent door, for any sound that will give me a clue as to why it's so bloody quiet around here. There's only the faint whisper of the wind blowing over the top of the high bank of snow curving protectively around me. But this wall only gives me the illusion of protection, it represents just a single stride in the path of a giant grizzly bear. There's no way that I'm going to be able to go to sleep tonight until I've checked the ridge for myself, in both directions. I look over the top of the high bank of snow, and down into the twilit valley below, only too fearful of what I might see. However my fears are unfounded. There's no movement of any kind in the valley below me. There's nothing to be seen moving along my trail either for as far as I can see along the ridge. Although, I doubt if a bear would be able to negotiate a ridge as narrow as this one.

I seal up the front opening to my tent. Then I remove my boots and place them in the bottom of my sleeping bag which should help to keep them from freezing during the night. I quickly follow my boots into the bag and snuggle down deep.

I came back to Alaska looking for an adventure. (Climbing in the European Alps had become far too routine for me.) Today, in the wilderness, I've had one, and tomorrow, well, I'll let it take care of itself.

I watch the flames on top of my gas stove pop, then dim, before gradually falling silent. I'm left alone in a freezing twilight. My hair and face, warm from the stove, gradually cool to match the temperature of the surrounding air. The chill deepens. I watch a fine layer of frost form on the thin transparent fabric of my inner tent. It starts out as a small round patch of ice surrounding the pole in the far corner of my tent. This circle of ice grows larger, then larger still, until it covers every sloping surface, exposed metal object, and dangly piece of string. I snuggle down deeper inside my sleeping bag. I'm lovely and warm all over now. I couldn't care less what Jack Frost does any more. I close my eyes.

I try to go to sleep, but I can't. My mind's still far too active. Instead, I mull over the events of the day and, to avoid thinking about the bear, I consider the aircraft I saw flying low over Mount Hess during the late after-noon. What perfect flying conditions the pilot had for his single-engine Cessna, before turning back towards what I assume was the settlement of Delta Junction. It definitely wasn't in the direction of Talkeetna, the more logical destination. Was it some "flightseeing" trip, with the usual complement of excited tourists on board? Then again perhaps it was ferrying in climbers. I can only hope that people are not coming to climb all over my mountain! A few climbers, that would be okay. But more than that? I desperately want to be alone here in the mountains. If I had wanted to meet other people I'd have gone climbing at some major centre in the European Alps. If a landing does take place on the glacier below Mount Hess, I'll just have to go and climb on some other mountain. I'll simply change my objec-tive. However, the Main West Fork Glacier is a very big one. A whole army of people could get lost up there. But why should I be so annoyed at the idea of meeting other people? Or is this a perfectly normal reaction for someone wanting to achieve an objective alone? I can't help but think how much easier my expedition would have been if I had flown in onto the glacier with all my food and equipment – but how much less the experi-ence.

With all the excitement of being so close to the real climbing, I'm almost forgetting the bear in the valley on the other side of the ridge. Why should I waste my time thinking about a bear? It doesn't concern me any more.

I must remember to tell some local hunter about the rogue bear in the Wells Creek area once I get back to Anchorage. It's too dangerous to leave one rampaging through the undergrowth like that. Ahead lies the real adventure in the mountains proper. I slowly drift off to sleep, to dream of giving names to unnamed routes, alone.

Chapter 3

Ice Ravine

I crawl out of my tent into the most beautiful day that I have ever experienced. Everything, as far as the eye can see, seems to sparkle in a shimmering display of light, just waiting for me to enter. I'm still in the shadow of the rock tower, but I'm coming, sun. I'm coming, as fast as I can. I had a safe night. I feel elated.

I climb up on top of the tower.

This is the first really fine detailed view I've had of the mountains ahead of me. It's a panoramic view, stretching out from horizon to horizon, and the three highest mountains, Mount Deborah, Mount Hess and Mount Hayes, lie central to it. Unfortunately, there's only the merest hint of Mount Hess, my objective, sticking out from behind the huge south-western face of Mount Deborah. It seems that I'm going to be kept in suspense right up to the very last moment. Although I've still got a very much foreshortened view of the Hayes group of mountains, they do live up to my highest expectations and are

35

well worth the effort of reaching this point in the expedition.

I should be entering the high mountains proper by tomorrow evening at the very latest, after completing my crossing of the wilderness. I think I'll alter my route here. The original plan was to walk the few remaining kilometres to the end of this ridge, to a small col just short of the narrow Nenana Glacier, in order to check that I'm on-route, then contour around the head of the swampy Monahan Flats before heading directly into the mountains bordering the Main West Fork Glacier. However, there appears to be a trail of sorts, starting at the base of this tower, then descending diagonally down the side of the ridge to a small lake on the Monahan Flats side. I can see it shimmering in the sun below me. The advantage of my new line is that it will provide me with a perfect time-saving short cut by removing the need to press on to the col. I only needed to go there to fix my position, but I can clearly see where I am now in these excellent conditions. Another advantage of my new line is that it will lead me directly into the mountains running along the side of the Main West Fork Glacier which have been my objective all along. Anything that will save me a great deal of wasted time and effort is well worth considering. But more to the point, if I alter my route now it will immediately place the high mountain ridge between myself and the bear. Perhaps I'm imagining a threat that does not exist. Who knows, only time will tell. But it's best if I take no chances.

I soon pack my equipment away. My cooking pans are already inside my rucksack. My sleeping bag has been folded up. There is just nine days' supply of food to be tied to the top of my sack in a green canvas kitbag. I soon have everything ready and take a careful last look around to make sure I've left nothing behind. I can't afford to be without a single item of food or equipment, so I stand quite still scrutinizing every tiny hollow in the snow around me.

There's an eerie silence still hanging over the ridge, but everything appears to be quite normal, up here and on my ascent route of the previous day. There's nothing to be seen moving down in the valley either. Perhaps it's time I livened things up?

Trundling!

That's the name given to this game in the climbing world. It only requires a steep mountain side and some really big boulders to make it all work. The larger they are the better.

I suppose it was Jane, the love of my life at the time, that started this craze for trundling when, in the summer of '79, on our first successful ascent of Mount Gerdine, in Alaska, Jane pushed John – the same John who is supporting me on this expedition – off the summit. He had tried to kiss her in their summit photograph and she had objected. John started a mini avalanche on the way down. Fortunately for us all, he survived. But anything that is good enough for Jane, conqueror of Mount Gerdine, is good enough for me. I start with a boulder, on the point of the ridge itself, rocking it back and forth. There's a tremendous crash as it strikes the snow slope below, its attendant avalanche continuing to roar down into the valley, picking up many more rocks and blocks of ice on the way. Another one suddenly takes off, started by the noise and movement of the first, with an audible thump that shakes the ground. What a marvellous way to start the day! But now I'm getting ambitious. Let's see if I can't find some really big boulders to push down into the valley. I walk carefully back along the ridge, stepping precisely into the steps that I made in the snow on the way up here, until brought to a halt by the second of the three rock towers.

Why shouldn't I try and topple it?

This second tower looks fragile enough, and about to fall over at any moment. Surely this can't be the same one that I climbed on the way up here yesterday? But this is definitely the same tower, the scratch marks made by my crampons are etched into the face of the rock. I could easily have got myself killed attempting such a climb. The fear of a bear following me had obviously blinded me to the dangers involved.

I place my hands inside an enormous crack which is the dominant feature on this side of the tower. It carries on right through. If only I could get my boots up inside the crack, as well as my hands, I might stand a chance of pushing the two halves of the tower apart and the smaller half down into the valley below. I reach up once more, stretching myself to the limit of my long reach now, trying to secure a good placement for both my hands inside the widest part of the crack. Once there I'll be able to pull myself up. Then I can get my boots to fit inside the crack, ready to push in opposite directions, trying to force the two halves of the tower apart.

The moment I get both feet inside the widest part of the crack, the walls begin to part, with the smaller half of the tower easily splitting away from the main bulk at the very few points where it was still connected. I'm surprised that any aspect of this great column of rock has remained standing for so long. I quickly drop a slab of pink granite down into the gap that has opened up between the two halves of the tower, to stop them from closing, and climb up inside what is now a small chimney. My main concern is to keep up the pressure on both walls to prevent them from closing up again. I begin to push even harder now, knowing that if I get it all wrong I could be dragged down into the valley along with the tower. I must be prepared to jump clear.

My concentration is broken by a loud crack, coming from somewhere deep within the base of the tower. The smaller half of the tower begins to sway very gently back and forth. Then there's another loud crack and I jump down out of the chimney into the snow. The tower is still fixed to the ridge. Surely it has got to fall. I can feel the ridge vibrating beneath my boots. Another violent tremor shakes it, then the smaller half of the tower topples over the edge of the ridge, easily splitting away from the main bulk, before bouncing and slamming into the snow slope below. Then the main bulk of the tower slowly starts to crumble at the base, before falling cleanly over the edge of the ridge. There's an enormous explosion as it hits the snow slope directly below me, debris begins to rain down everywhere, landing on top of the trees in the valley, flattening the bushes, sweeping all before it.

"Beat that one, Jane!" I shout out loud.

Before I leave, I tear a page out of my notebook to leave a message for future climbers.

I, David Fletcher, passed this way, heading for the side of the Main West Fork Glacier, then on to climb Mount Hess, alone. Avoid the valley below, (on the Mount McKinley side of the ridge, the west side) like the plague. I think there's a rogue bear down there in the Wells Creek area. I can't be absolutely sure that there's one there, but either way, there's something very evil and sinister about the place. If you descended from this ridge by way of Monahan Flats (on the east side of the ridge) in order to get back to the Denali Highway, you're bound to get your feet wet out on the Flats, and you'll definitely get a large number of mosquito bites during the late summer months, but you'll be a great deal safer.

Good Luck!

David Fletcher.

I fold the message up, and place it inside an empty tin can which I hammer into a sheltered crack on the overhanging, sunny side of the tower. This should keep my message dry. I wonder if anyone will ever find it? Out here, in this vast empty Alaskan wilderness, who knows?

Following my new traverse line on the Monahan Flats side of the ridge, I start to slide my way smoothly over the surface of the snow, using my boots like a very efficient pair of skis, heading down towards the lake. The snow is a perfect consistency today for glissading high on this sunny side of the ridge. It beats the shit out of walking any day. But my speed suddenly increases with a frightening rapidity when I hit a patch of smooth snow. Then almost immediately after striking this first patch I hit another. The wind streaks through my hair now. Then it starts to tear at my clothing. Such exhilaration! Such power! Such a wonderful feeling of total freedom! I decide, against my better judgement and all the rules of common sense, not to slow down. Why on earth should I do that? I came to Alaska to have fun. I lean to the right, then I tilt my body over to the left, gently criss-crossing my new trail, heading down towards the lake, executing numerous shallow stem turns on the way. But I must stop to rest soon. I've a long way to go today. I break to a gentle stop to regain my breath and composure.

I let my rucksack fall from my shoulders into the snow behind me. The full weight of all my heavy equipment hits the slope with a thud and my feet almost float up off the ground now I've been relieved of my burden. There are numerous creatures on the slopes opposite. I sit down on top of my rucksack and shade my eyes against the full glare of the sun, trying to decide what they are. Surely they must be caribou and part of the huge Nelchina herd, one of the thirteen major reindeer herds roaming Alaska. They usually move up onto the higher tundra slopes at the beginning of the summer months, to feed on lichens assorted plants and shrubs, after spending the long winter months down in the forests bordering the Parks and Denali Highways. Every available patch of snow seems to be occupied with caribou today. They could be here to escape the swarms of warble flies that cover most of the lower ground at this time of year. There must be plenty of biting insects out on the flats today, if the caribou up here are anything to go by. Caribou herds are rarely as relaxed as this one. Usually they are on the move, in a never ending search for food. Today this group is in a very relaxed state, which can only mean one thing, that there are no big predators, like bears, in the area. That makes me feel a great deal safer, because I'm going to be headed in their direction soon.

I decide to walk the remaining short distance down towards the lake. I'd rather move slowly, playing it safe for once, than glissade and risk falling. It's just a matter of placing one foot below the other, and being very careful not to slip in the deteriorating snow conditions at these lower levels.

The lake, shimmering in the sun just a short distance below me, tempts me for a swim. But it would be too dangerous to stop here. There are far too many animal tracks in the snow around the shore for my liking, with most of them converging on the northern tip of the lake. This area is clearly a major passing point. The paw and hoof prints of most types of animals are represented here in the snow, mostly caribou and moose, yet it's the full larger paw prints of the Alaskan brown bears that worry me the most.

I begin to descend less steeply now towards the river coming directly from the snout of the Nenana Glacier, still out of sight several kilometres to the north, and I cross over to the far bank. I don't know why I feel so pleased with myself. Or is it that I've reached an important stage in the expedition – no more rivers to cross. River crossings are a major cause of accidents in the wilderness.

I think this is as good a place as any to rest up before continuing on into the hills bordering the Main West Fork Glacier. I doubt I'll have many more opportunities like this for sorting and drying my equipment out, my schedule's far too tight. My washing line, a nylon cord stretched between two tent poles, makes a colourful spectacle. I lie back, with my knees up, on top of a warm riverside rock to watch my shirts, socks and woollen jumpers steaming in the sun. It's a pretty blaze of royal blue, red and opulent green. I could lie here all day beside the Nenana watching the contents of my washing line steaming in the sun. But what if an aircraft were to fly directly overhead? The pilot could easily mistake the colourful contents of my washing line for an emergency SOS. That would put an end to my expedition.

I'll just have to be prepared to take everything down at the first sign of an aircraft approaching.

I check to see if my clothing has dried. The cuffs of my red down jacket are still wet, the result of thrusting my ice-axe into the snow behind me to safeguard myself from slipping. The wrists of both woollen jumpers are just as bad. I'll leave my clothing where it is for the moment. I've still got some time to spare – and dream. I wonder whether there is any gold in this river. Almost every major river in Alaska will contain at least some trace of colour – those tiny telltale flakes of gold. Perhaps one day I shall return to my home city of Kingston-upon-Hull with a smile on my face and a twinkle in my eye, the only signs to betray the fact that I have discovered gold.

I think I'll have a shave. I've never felt quite right until I've had one at least some time during the day. My shaving mirror fits neatly into place inside a small indentation on the sunny side of a boulder. Every detail on the ground behind me shows up quite clearly in it. There's my long line of boot prints to be seen in the snow, stretching back across the Nenana River, past the boulder field where the snout of the retreating Nenana Glacier used to be, then past the lake, leading diagonally up to the crest of the ridge and the site of my bivouac last night beneath the tower. I can see the glass-like surface of the water beneath this ridge quite clearly, which is remarkable considering the distance involved here. Just below the lake there's a small movement to be seen. The sight of anything at all moving up there almost throws me into a panic. I quickly turn around, almost knocking my shaving mirror flying, as I scan the length and breadth of my trail, cupping my hands over my eyes in a desperate attempt to see what kind of creature it is that's moving down by the lake. But it's hopeless trying to see anything when faced with the full glare of the sun reflected up off the snow. (It's moments like this when I regret not bringing a pair of binoculars.) I can definitely see something moving down by the lake now.

The quieter it becomes the more I start to worry. As I continue my journey up into the mountains bordering the Main West Fork Glacier, I keep stopping to look behind me, but there's no creature to be seen. There are no unusual noises either. Even the river, still relatively close to me in the bottom of the valley, has calmed down since I crossed over. There's only the faint whisper of the wind in my ears now, and the sharp crackle of ice under my feet each time I step forward up the slope.

The mountains gradually begin to tower above me. The higher I climb up the valley, the stronger the wind becomes. I can't believe its strength now, and the direction it is coming from. It has blown in my face on all my previous expeditions to Alaska. But now it is behind me, trying to push me and my load up into the mountains for hour after hour. There is a fast flowing stream to my left and one of similar strength to my right. I think I'll take the right-hand fork. My chosen stream leads me up into a narrowing valley with towering walls of ice on either side. I doubt if this place has ever seen the summer sun for any reasonable length of time, let alone another human being, although this can't be at all unusual for such a remote and high elevation. I'm happy to be surrounded by an eternity of winter nights now.

The valley continues to narrow until it begins to look more like a ravine. Then suddenly there's nowhere else left to go. I've reached the head of the ravine. I'm left in a dead-end world of frozen waterfalls that surround me to protect me, to make me feel safe. This is just the place I've been seeking. I pitch my tent close to the bank of the stream in the head of the ravine and spread my equipment out inside it. Now I'm free to explore the possibility of climbing out of the ravine which is what I've got to do early tomorrow morning.

I walk slowly and carefully around the circular head of the ravine, jumping the stream twice on each complete circuit. I'm in my element, as only a climber can be, surrounded by these vertical walls of ice. I probe with the pick of my ice-axe, looking for the slightest sign of weakness, oblivious to the cold surrounding me. All my concentration is being channelled into finding a route up to the top of the ravine wall. Will I be able to climb this great twenty-four-metre curtain of ice, curving smoothly around the circular head of the ravine? A guidebook for the area doesn't exist. Anyway, the build up of ice will never be the same each year. There's only my ability as a climber to trust in here. It's this confidence in my power to see the job through that carries me forward towards the section of the waterfall where the ice is most pronounced. I doubt if my route will turn out to be the hardest one around, or the easiest, but it will be my chosen Waterfall Route. If I succeed, I'll leave the rope in place to make my departure easier when it's time to leave at midnight.

I begin to climb straight up the almost vertical wall of ice, towards what appears from below to be a neat square-cut top at the higher limit of the waterfall. The ice steepens considerably. I reach high above my head with my ice-axe held tightly in my right hand. I stab at the ice with its pick and follow this with several more short sharp stabbing movements with the pick of my ice-hammer, grasped in my other hand. Then I step up the ice once more, kicking forward into the brittle substance each time, with the front-points on my crampons only just managing to hold me in place. The quality of the ice suddenly takes a change for the worse. It begins to splinter away from around my crampons each time I step up the wall. I can clearly hear small fragments striking the rocks in the bed of the ravine below me. It's reasuring to hear this noise because my ability to see the ground is restricted: at least I know that it still exists. I continue to make good progress, both axes ringing out loud and clear on the hollow surface of the waterfall. But pleasant though these sounds are, the ice is telling me in no uncertain terms that it's not going to stay glued to the rock forever. I'm totally committed to climbing out of the ravine now. It's going to be extremely difficult, if not

47

impossible, for me to reverse my route. All I ask is that the ice stays firm until I reach the top. Then it can do what it likes.

I must have reached a point at least halfway up the waterfall. As if on cue, a small rock appears, jutting out from beneath the ice, enabling me to stand up in comfort so that I can place a runner to belay myself. I quickly cut a small notch in the ice. Then I tap the end of a long tubular ice-screw into the hole. Just a few gentle blows are all that's needed to get it firmly embedded. Then I place the pick of my ice-axe into the eye of the ice-screw and I screw it firmly home. A large screw-gate karabiner clipped into the eye of the ice-screw is all that's needed now to get my rope running smoothly through this runner. This running belay placed at a point more than halfway up the waterfall should prevent me from hitting the floor of the ravine if I fall off. It gives me a great feeling of security, even though I'm very aware that an ice-screw is only as strong as the ice into which it has been placed. As I continue climbing I'm in for a pleasant surprise, the angle is easing off. The climbing will still require care, but the tension has gone out of it now. My rope quickly follows on behind me, up the last few metres of brittle ice. I step very carefully over the edge of the waterfall, with my legs cramping up and my lungs gasping for breath, swaying momentarily on the long spikes of my crampons protruding from beneath my boots. I must not slip. I've got a long way to fall if I come off now.

For the first time I can now see back down my complete route, from the lowest point down by the river, to my tent pitched close to the bank of the stream in the head of the ravine. It looks so small down there, just a tiny splash of shiny green colour in a brilliant white landscape. The all too pleasant gravel bars, fast flowing streams and boulder slopes are gone now, mostly covered over with snow. There are no more sparkling quartzite veins, glittering up at me out of the rocks to light my way. Everything colourful has vanished under a freezing cold blanket of snow. There's nothing but snow and ice all around me now, from valley floor to mountain top. It shows me far more clearly than anything else ever could, that I'm getting close to my high peak destination, Mount Hess.

I'm tempted into carrying on up the snow slope at the top of the ravine wall. I might even be able to reach the crest of the ridge above me before nightfall for a view down onto the Main West Fork Glacier. But I'm far too tired to proceed any further. I'll save my remaining energy for one really good push forward tomorrow morning. There'll be plenty of time to take in the full savage beauty of the glacier then. But for now there's only one place to be and that's back inside my tent where food, warmth and sleep await.

I abseil back down the full length of the waterfall, unclipping my rope from the runner placed halfway up. I've got a single continuous rope in place now, hanging straight down the wall of the ravine.

There's just one last task to perform before I settle in

for the night. I must cache some food for the return journey. I know full well that if I don't make an attempt to bury it now I'll never get around to doing it in the rush to get away early tomorrow morning. There's two days' supply to be left here in the bed of the ravine, the minimum amount necessary to get me safely back to the Denali Highway. The recommended cache for food is up a tree, but tundra slopes are by definition treeless. So I sweat with the effort of rolling granite boulders into place, building my cairn. A bear can easily sniff out a free food parcel from a distance of several kilometres, though I doubt if one would be able to move the magnificent cairn of stones placed directly over my food cache. What an enormous expenditure of energy it takes to raise it. But I'm happy at the end result.

My gas stove has warmed the air inside my tent. I need this if I'm to motivate myself sufficiently to sit up inside my sleeping bag and sort out the rest of my equipment. There's not a great deal to go with me tomorrow, my approach will be to travel light and climb fast. Speed is the key to success on any venture, but this is only possible if you are very fit and are carrying only the essentials by way of equipment. The essentials still include climbing helmet, a few rock pitons, ice-screws, karabiners, rope slings, ice-axe and ice-hammer, crampons, map, whistle, compass, headtorch and batteries. Food will be the heaviest item. There are six days' supply, tied to the top of my rucksack in the green canvas kitbag. It would be heavier still if it weren't in freeze-dried form. Just add water.

I must repair the bindings on my left snowshoe, a task put off for far too long. It's a simple matter of joining the two severed parts with a small rivet. This shiny silver bolt makes an excellent join. The strap, though shorter now, looks and feels as good as new. They have performed remarkably well. I can't help but think that this is due more to the fact that they are flexible rather than any other factor. The Inuit got it right: a narrow snowshoe, that will bend without breaking, designed for hunting and running, and a broad one for back-packing heavy loads, just like mine.

The remaining straps and buckles on my snowshoes are all in good working order. There are no visible cracks in the metal frames on my crampons. The picks on both my axes are sharp. Survival is all about checking every item of equipment, then doing it again, taking nothing at face value, trying to reduce the odds against yourself, and never more so than when you are climbing alone.

I set the alarm on my wrist-watch for midnight, a time when the snow will be frozen solid. This will give me the longest period with the best possible climbing conditions. It was the numerous avalanche cones that I saw on the slopes around me yesterday that have convinced me of the necessity to climb during the colder night hours. But it won't be dark then. The sun only dips below the horizon for a few hours each night at this high northern latitude, so there will be plenty of light to climb by. From now on, I've decided to do all my climbing, where possible, during the night, sleeping during the day in any natural shelter that I can find. I've also decided to leave my tent where it is in the bed of the ravine. I'll bury it next to my food cache and pick it up on my return. My tent will be a very definite weight off my shoulders.

I can see the sky quite clearly now through the small ventilation hole in the roof. The clouds and mist, so much in evidence today, have all but disappeared. All day I've waited for them to clear up completely, and now that I'm back inside my tent, ready to go to sleep, the sky clears. Still, there's always tomorrow, and I've no reason to believe that it won't be a fine day. At the very least a clear sky tonight will mean a wonderful crisp hard snow in the morning, just perfect for climbing.

I am so tired after my exertions that even a far distant howling noise cannot keep me awake.

Chapter 4

Within Claws' Reach?

There's no wind to contend with today as I dismantle the tent. I squash the material, frost flying everywhere, into my green nylon stuff sack. I'll bury it later on – next to my food cache.

It's reassuring to see my rope hanging straight down the waterfall. But I can't afford to waste a single precious moment admiring it in these near perfect climbing conditions. I quickly clip my jumar clamps onto my rope. Each joins me into the front of my sit-harness and small tape ladders going down to my boots. I bounce up and down on the end of my rope once more, before pushing my jumar clamps up the single rope towards the top of the waterfall. I revel in my new found freedom. I feel happy at the close-to-midnight mist brushing gently up against my skin. I'm ecstatic as only a climber can be at leaving the ground behind. I smile. At least there are no worries about dislodging loose rock on this wall, it's snow and ice all the way.

I continue my smooth ascent without incident, up and then over the edge of the waterfall and remove my snowshoes from around my shoulders, bending over almost double to do so. This leaves my hands free to begin pulling my rucksack up on the end of my rope. Small gaps appear in the mist from time to time, enabling me to see my sack, securely tied to the end of my rope, in the bed of the ravine. It looks so small down there as I begin to haul it up the waterfall in a sweating, heaving, hand over hand motion that leaves me gasping for breath.

I can't for the life of me see why climbers glamorize this sack-hauling procedure, seeing it as an easy way of transporting a heavy load up a wall. It's more the lesser of two evils, easier to haul than to carry, but still requiring a great deal of hard physical effort, and not without its drawbacks.

One such disadvantage occurs now.

My rope suddenly stops moving upwards with a shock that almost pulls me over the edge, skating about in my crampons until the front-points catch on some pebbles embedded in the ice. My rucksack must have got caught on some projection sticking out of the ice. I take an extra turn of my rope around a boulder, then begin to pull with all the strength and determination at my disposal. It's becoming almost impossible to lift my rucksack now. If anything it seems to be pulling me rather than the other way around. What the hell has gone wrong with all my carefully laid sack-hauling procedures? The mist has closed in once more to complicate proceedings. When I lean out over the edge of the waterfall in a desperate attempt to catch sight of where my rucksack is stuck, it's no use. All I can see is my rope vanishing below me into the mist.

The mist is getting worse, swirling all around me, and into the hidden gullies and buttresses, caressing the icy slabs and filling the ravine from top to bottom with a fine almost impenetrable barrier of water vapour.

There's nothing but the top six metres or so of my rope to be seen now. I can't stand here all day holding onto it. I've got to do something positive about my rucksack. I expect it to jam every now and again when pulling it up a rock wall. I don't expect it to get stuck on some relatively smooth Alaskan ice. Unless, of course, it's gone and got itself caught up on the eye of the ice-screw I placed halfway yesterday. How on earth do I free it now, unless I lower it back down the wall and then try to pull it up again?

I give another frustrated tug and the full weight of my heavy rucksack suddenly comes back onto my arms. I don't hesitate, and haul it in, smoothly and powerfully this time, until it suddenly appears over the edge of the waterfall. At least my ice-axes have survived the ordeal intact, securely tied to the top by a long nylon strap. They could have easily been ripped off in the struggle. One side has a number of long tears running from top to bottom. I'll simply mend them later on tonight, all five of them. As for the ice-screw, which I've decided was probably the culprit, it could have worked itself loose and be sticking out proud of

55

the ice. I'll just have to file it down at the first opportunity.

I prepare to abseil back down into the ravine. There's my tent to be buried, then the ice-screw to be removed on the way back up my rope. Then I've got to locate the side of the Main West Fork Glacier. All these differing thoughts run through my mind, filling my consciousness and clouding out my normally sound judgement and the plain and simple truth that only a set of razor-sharp claws could have made those rips in the side of my rucksack.

I begin to abseil down into the ravine. My crampons crash hard into the ice each time they hit the glassy surface of the waterfall. Another wonderful burst of unexpected energy suddenly overtakes me and the ice splinters out in all directions. I pause just short of the floor of the ravine, enjoying spinning around, near the end of my rope, just a short distance above the ground; face in to the ice, then out to the mist, then in to the ice again. To this day I cannot figure out why I decide to pause here. My spin continues, a very slow and deliberate one now, as I'm coming to a stop. In to face the ice, out to the mist, in to the ice, out to the parting mist – and the enormous dark shadow crouched low behind the pile of stones covering my food cache.

I stop my spin. There are only the two front-points on the toe of my left climbing boot to hold me in place now. This is my only contact with the waterfall and reality. I remain facing into the wall. I daren't turn around to see what kind of creature it is that's hiding behind my cairn. This small section of highly polished ice seems to command my full and undivided attention. I can't bear to look at the enormous shadow being reflected back at me out of the ice any more. I close my eyes. I freeze in absolute utter horror, while every one of my senses screams out at me to turn around and look behind me.

But I still dare not turn around.

I remain facing into the waterfall, with my eyes closed, trembling with fear, not daring to breathe. There's not a whisper to be heard anywhere. It's as if the very silence itself is to be a guarantee of my safety. So long as I keep my eyes closed everything is going to be all right.

But I know full well that I've got to turn around and look sooner or later, because whatever it is that's over there might have left by now and be creeping up behind me! Even though I know all this, I still hesitate to act. I keep clinging to the false belief that the very silence itself and my closed eyelids will keep me safe from harm. I continue to wait like an ostrich with its head buried deep in the sand, hoping beyond hope for a miracle to occur, waiting until I can wait no more. Fear drives me to act.

I allow the two front-points on my left crampon to slide slowly down off the ice, and around I go, facing out to the mist, and when I open my eyes, I find myself looking into the face of the bear. It has to be the one whose cub I killed. I can tell by the hatred written all over it. There's a terrible scar cutting diagonally down across the bear's entire face: almost severing its nose completely. What a ferocious battle this bear must have fought to receive such a wound.

Heaven help me now!

Scar Face lies crouched down just a short distance away across the other side of the stream, looking like some monster from another world, with its hideous features, head low to the ground, muscles taut and ready to spring forward at any moment now. Yet it remains quite still, hardly moving a muscle, just watching, and waiting for God knows what. The dark brown fur is clearly visible against the snow plastering the far ravine wall. It silhouettes only too well the greasy hump of matted hair, knotted tissue and gristle, the unmistakable sign of a grizzly bear. This hump rises above one of the largest pair of shoulders that I have ever seen. But it's the awesome combination of those two terrible words, grizzly bear, now drilling their way deep into my brain, that terrifies me the most. They send a huge shock wave of fear running down through my body. Why can't it be a black bear, or even a normal brown one. But no, it has to be a giant grizzly bear.

Memories return of tales told me by that friend and hunter on my first ever trip to Alaska. There was the musher, caught in his sleeping bag, trapped there when his dogs ran back to him for protection. His friends found only his left foot. Then the terrible story of the trapper who thought he was safe inside his log cabin. The grizzly came in through the walls and ate him, boots, bible, furs and all. There was only a gold wedding ring left to identify his remains. I am now staring into the scarred face of the most feared animal on this earth; and it is staring long and hard back at me; just a mere stone's throw away across the other side of the stream. The bear's eyes are boring into me now, they seem to be flashing out a message of sheer unforgiving hatred. Yet terrible though that stare is, I can't help but feel mesmerized by the sheer beauty of being face to face with the perfect killing machine!

But I'm still petrified at the sight of all that hatred pouring out towards me.

"I swear to God I meant no harm! I truly swear!" The words coming out of my mouth, of course, have no effect at all on the bear. I now know for sure that one of us is going to die.

I'm clearly within reach of the bear's long forelegs, if it were to decide to charge forward towards me and make a grab for my legs. I feel sure that it is going to do just that at any moment. I can't remain hanging on near the end of my rope forever. I'd rather die now, trying to escape, than wait to be eaten alive.

I slowly reach up, high above my head, with my left hand, ready to pull myself up my rope to reach the safer ground at the top of the high ravine wall. I should be safe from the bear on top of the waterfall. But even though I'm concentrating fully now on trying to get my left hand as high as possible up my rope, before I make any serious move to escape, I still daren't take my eyes off the bear's evil snarling face. Even though it still hasn't shown any sign yet that it has noticed my left hand, almost at full stretch now, slowly moving up my rope. (My right hand is still holding me in place on my descendeur.) But I'm going to need both of them free if I'm to effectively pull myself up my rope. Even though I know all this, I still hesitate to act further, fear holds me back. I feel sure that once I make that first move to escape, that movement will, of itself, force the issue, and that the bear will come charging forward towards me. *Dear God! Why do I have to be so terribly afraid?*

The wind suddenly starts to blow into the ravine from somewhere lower down in the main valley. This cooling breeze hits me full in the face and breaks the tension – at least something is happening now. Then it begins to clear the mist. But the wind, so welcome and refreshing at first, starts me swinging back and forth, hanging on near the end of my rope.

These are gentle swings at first, going from left to right, then back again, nothing more, with my left leg still held straight out in front of me, to prevent me from turning around. I remain hanging on my rope, first going one way, then the other, still trying to pluck up the courage to climb higher. Back and forth, near the end of my rope. Still hanging on in fear of the great bear.

Then one of my karabiners, looped into the back of my waist-belt on the end of its long tape sling, suddenly strikes the ice. In rebounding off the hard surface, it effectively takes the timing of any decision I have to make out of my hands. The silence hanging down over the ravine suddenly breaks.

There's just the smallest of taps to be heard at first from the karabiner striking the ice, then an almost continuous tap-tap-tapping noise ringing out loudly in my ears, echoing off the high sanctuary walls, as my karabiner strikes the ice harder, then harder still!

The bear blinks.

I'm almost caught by surprise by the movement, and nearly jump out of my skin, but my karabiner, oblivious to any movement at all by the bear, carries on tapping out more loudly and noisily than ever before. I make an instinctive grab for it. I've got to prevent the thing striking the ice again. In my panic to take hold of it, I forget about keeping still, the only thoughts in my mind being to stop all this noise. But my karabiner is fast becoming the very least of all my worries.

The bear suddenly raises itself up out of the snow to a height of well over three metres. Then it bounds forward in my direction. One monstrous stride and it is across to my side of the stream and running in a fully erect posture, just like a man would do, straight towards me.

I react instinctively now.

I drop my descendeur. (It remains swinging on my rope directly below me.) I grasp hold of my rope with both hands. I can clearly see that the bear has every intention of tearing me to pieces. I start to climb up my rope. Just a bit further will do. That's all it will take to get my legs safely out of the bear's long reach. I must at all costs get as high as I can before it arrives at the bottom of the waterfall. Every second is going to count here.

Suddenly the first huge hammer blows strike the ice directly below me. But it won't be able to reach me now. The huge paws and forelegs of the great bear continue to slam into the ice a short distance below my boots. Just how much damage the waterfall will be able to sustain before it eventually collapses, I don't know. The complete sheet of ice plastering the rock begins to vibrate. I'm sure I can feel it moving in front of me.

Then some large pieces of ice begin to fall down from somewhere high above me at the very top edge of the high ravine wall. Most of this debris falls harmlessly well over to one side of me. But my ice-screw is just a short distance above me now. I must clip myself into it before I do anything else. I reach up once more. I'm almost there. I quickly pull myself level with my running belay. Then I clip a large screw-gate karabiner into the eye of the ice-screw. There's a loud click as the gate snaps shut. I remain resting on the end of the short tape sling clipped into the eye of the ice-screw for some time. I must get my breath back. I've got to avoid the heaviest lumps of ice, still falling down from somewhere high above me. But most of all, I'm trying to avoid the bear's long claws slicing through the air, just a short distance below my boots.

I'm fortunate here in that this last shower of ice misses me completely. However, the bear receives the full force of all this debris upon its head and shoulders. The largest lumps of ice seem to explode upon impact with the bear's massive chest. But it simply shrugs them off as if they were little more than a fine sifting of angel dust, the first light snow of winter. The bear looks up at me once more. For a savage fleeting moment our eyes meet. I can see that nothing has changed, there's still the same awful expression on the bear's snarling face.

The bear roars up at me, deep-throated, all-encompassing, powerful, so sure of itself now, so certain of the outcome.

I watch horrified as it backs away from the bottom of the wall. What on earth is it going to do now? The bear stops just a few metres out from the ice. Then it bounds forward, standing up almost immediately. Then it begins to slam its two huge front paws into the ice directly below me. The complete sheet of ice plastering the rock suddenly begins to vibrate once more. I start to bounce in and out from the wall, still looped into the thin tape sling, clipped into the eye of the ice-screw, placed halfway up the waterfall.

More ice begins to fall down from somewhere out of sight, high above. These are just small pieces compared with the last huge avalanche. But what if the complete sheet of ice plastering the rock gives way? I'm going to end up, along with the rest of the ice, in a heap in the bed of the ravine. My only chance of escaping from here is to climb up my rope to the top of the wall. But I'm never going to be able to climb the complete distance using my arms alone – not after all my initial rope-climbing attempts. I'm going to need both my jumar clamps clipped onto my rope if I'm ever going to climb out of here and it's too late to get them organized.

A loud splintering noise begins to come from some-where. I look around me now in a state of complete and utter panic. Where on earth is this new noise coming from? The question is soon answered when a wide crack opens up in the ice directly below my boots. I watch it race across the ice, in both directions, on either side of me. This crack is clearly going to split the top half of the waterfall from the bottom half, dividing it into two enormous sheets of ice. It can't possibly go any further now after travelling around the complete head of the ravine. Then the enormous sheet of ice, only a metre or so beneath me, comprising the complete lower half of the waterfall, slowly begins to peel backwards, landing on top of the screaming bear.

I'm left hanging on the end of my thin tape sling in a state of complete and utter shock.

I can't believe what has happened . . .

There's only the finest velvet flutter of fast settling snow dust to be heard around me now. Then silence. The enormous plume of snow dust, created by the avalanche when it hit the floor of the ravine, begins to drift up past me – blotting out the chaos all around me. I can't see a thing now.

The cloud eventually settles back down, filling in the gaps between the huge blocks of ice now littering the floor of the ravine.

A scene of utter chaos greets me. There's nothing but a great mass of snow and ice in the bed of the ravine. This debris extends all the way back across to the other side of the stream, only just missing my food cache cairn, and under it all there's the bear. The final few remaining small particles of airborne snow dust settle.

The bear must be dead under all this debris.

I mustn't forget that I entered the ravine in order to bury my tent. I must not get distracted in any way from accomplishing my objective. But I think I'll stay hanging on my rope a little while longer. It would be all too easy for me to make a wrong decision. I've got to think very carefully about my next move. I remain hanging on my rope, sitting down in my sit-harness, for some time, joined into the ice-screw by the thin tape sling, placed halfway up the waterfall, still attached to my rope by my descendeur.

I'm only thankful that I'm still alive.

My tent seems to have survived the avalanche intact, rolling about on top of a slab of ice, still packed inside its green nylon stuff sack. The wind blows it first one way, then the other, always seeming to stop just that little bit short of disaster, never quite gaining the momentum necessary to fall out of reach. I decide to play it safe. I'll leave the tent where it is. I can always pick it up later on. I've got to enter the ravine again on the way back in order to retrieve my food supplies buried beneath the cairn.

However, like so many of my plans on this expedition, no sooner do I make them than . . .

The great jumble of ice littering the floor of the ravine begins to move, first a wicked-looking claw appears from beneath the chaos, then another, then a leg, then a head, then an enormous, muscle-bound chest breaks free of the debris.

The bear gradually stands up on its rear legs. Then it begins to shake itself down, seemingly utterly contemptuous of everything around it. Then, without pausing for a single moment, it bounds forward towards me, brushing aside several large blocks of snow and ice on the way, as if they weren't there at all.

I can see only too clearly just what it intends to do next. My legs are still dangling down dangerously close to the ground.

The bear breaks to a furious halt just a few metres below me. I can see that it has every intention of hooking its claws into my legs and pulling me down. I've got to get higher. Just a short distance further on up my rope will do. But the bear doesn't wait. It springs up what is now the rock wall beneath me. I'm almost caught by surprise by this sudden monstrous leap. Fortunately for me, its claws miss my legs, slicing harmlessly well over to one side of me this time. I lift them even higher, hugging my knees close to my chest. I'll remain in this position for as long as it takes. But the blast of air from the bear's massive paws slicing past me hits me like a powerful gust of wind. I'm blown well over to one side of the ice-screw, still connected into the end of the short tape sling. This same blast of air also starts my climbing rope oscillating wildly. Then the ice-screws hanging down from my waist-belt begin to ring out loud as they collide with one another. I struggle to clip one jumar clamp onto the rope above me. I'm connected into my rope now, as well as the ice-screw. I can't help but feel safer. But I'm going to need both my jumar clamps clipped onto the rope above me if I'm ever going to climb out of here. I must somehow get my second one fixed in place as quickly as possible. But each time I reach up my rope, with my remaining jumar clamp held tightly in my right hand, I fail to lock it into place. My hands, normally so sure in every movement that they make, just will not stop shaking. I miss the rope once more. The spiked cam keeps on closing onto thin air, anywhere but onto the waiting rope.

God damn it! Shit!

The bear begins to pound on the wall beneath me now. It has apparently given up trying to hook me down. It snarls up at me once more, its hot putrid breath condensing into misshapen ice crystals on the rugged hairs around the edges of its jaws. Then it screams a savage blood-curdling scream up at me; one of absolute utter frustration and fury.

My only chance of getting out of here lies in my being able to clip my remaining jumar clamp onto the rope. I can't keep my legs raised up to my chest indefinitely. I glance down at the bear once more. There are some terrible noises coming out of its throat now.

The bear remains directly below me, first screaming, then pounding on the rock wall alternately with its two massive front paws. It's a wild and frenzied drum beat. I try to ignore the noise. But I can't. The noise is everywhere.

67

All I have to do is pull back the tiny aluminium cam that holds the rope tight in the jumar clamp, then clip it onto the rope. It's as simple as that. The trouble is that nothing's that simple when working under pressure. Perhaps if I tried opening the aluminium cam with my teeth this time? I manage to hold it open for a few seconds longer than normal. I quickly lean in towards the rope. The aluminium tastes so tinny in my mouth, so metallic, this cold and frosty morning. I'm almost there now. I even manage to smile.

But it seems to infuriate the bear still further. It responds by jumping up the wall beneath me and managing to hook its claws into the heel of my left climbing boot. I drop my remaining jumar clamp in fright as a red hot knife-like pain shoots up through my left leg. The jumar remains swinging on the end of a thin tape sling directly below me. Good God! My leg feels as if it's being torn away from the rest of my body!

Heaven help me now!

I should never have taken my eyes off the bear. It starts to pull me out from the ice. The pain travelling up through my left leg is indescribable. My head starts to spin around . . . I can feel myself slowly sinking into unconsciousness. I feel sick. But I've got to fight this nauseous feeling. I must never give in to the bear.

I grip my rope even tighter. Then I start to pull myself up in a last desperate attempt to break free. I must pull myself away from its vicious grasp. But without both my jumar clamps attached to my rope

I'm never going to succeed. I can't seem to get a grip at all now. I can feel all the energy draining out of my arms. If I don't pull myself away from the bear I will have had it. I can't hold onto my rope forever. The bear's claws suddenly rip out of the heel of my left climbing boot. I fall back, face first, into the ice, the front crash bar on my climbing helmet saving me from serious injury, although nothing seems to hurt any more. Perhaps I'm far too numb with shock to really care what happens to me.

The bear soon regains its feet after falling backwards into the dry stream bed in the head of the ravine. I hoped that it had broken its bloody neck, but no such luck. It quickly returns to the fray with a savage silent teeth-bared growl.

I don't need any motivating now. I quickly pull my remaining jumar in, clip it onto the rope and begin to climb up towards the top of the high ravine wall, oblivious of the pain in my left leg.

The top of the wall comes into sight. I climb over the edge of the waterfall. I let go of both my jumar clamps, which remain hanging on the rope directly below me, and I stagger forward up the slope, pulling myself, hand over hand up my rope still anchored securely to the boulder at the top of the wall. I lie down in the snow and look up at the mist floating all around me. I feel exhausted. I feel shattered. But I'm glad to be alive.

I wipe the sweat from my forehead with the back of my silk glove. The finely woven material feels warm on my skin this morning. But my thoughts are far away from warm silk gloves and pleasant sensations. Instead they're on the ordeal I've just endured. I never want to see another bear again for as long as I live. Every last one should be rounded up and dumped on some remote island in the middle of the Bering Strait.

The end of my rope suddenly appears in my hands. I must have been pulling it in all along. It's strange but I don't seem to remember doing that. Shock. The end has been damaged by the bear, about three metres in all. I'll simply cut off the torn section. I'll still have enough left to climb on.

It's a relief to be lying down doing nothing. But my peace and tranquillity are soon shattered by a tremendous commotion coming from somewhere deep within the confines of the ravine. What on earth is the bear doing now?

Curiosity gets the better of me. I crawl forward on my hands and knees towards the edge of the ravine wall. I've not the slightest intention of letting the bear see me. I peep down over the edge of the waterfall. The bear must be mad! It is slowly tearing my tent to pieces in its jaws. My curses I have to whisper very quietly, for I must not draw any undue attention to myself. Small pieces of shiny green material are being blown all over the floor of the ravine. If only I'd buried it when I got up this morning instead of putting it off till later. Still, I'm not going to rely on my tent for shelter any more. It's snow caves for me from now on, all the way.

I turn my attention to the heel of my left climbing boot. Blood is still seeping out of one of the eyelet holes at the very bottom of my gaiter. There's a single claw mark cutting down through the heel unit. The bear's claws must have caught on the metal stiffening shank running the length of my boot. That explains how it was able to pull me out from the wall. My left foot still hurts like hell, but that's the extent of my injuries that I can feel. Perhaps I'd better take my boot off now, just to make absolutely certain that my foot is okay. I kneel down in the snow . . .

But then I think I'd better not remove anything, at least not up here, just in case the bear has already managed to figure out a way around to the top of the high ravine wall. That single thought more than any other fills me with a terrible fear. Up until this moment I'd felt safe on top of the waterfall, but I don't feel that way any more.

There are just two choices left open to me, both having fatal flaws built into them. My first and most obvious one is to run for it and try and reach the safety of the Main West Fork Glacier before the bear catches up with me. I doubt if it would pursue me for any distance out onto the ice. The problem with this course of action is that it might already have figured out a way around to the top of the high ravine wall and catch me up before I reach the glacier. My second option is to wait up here on top of the wall. If the bear finds a way round to come after me, I abseil down into the ravine. If it still persists in following me, then I jumar back up my rope to the top of the waterfall. However, this is a game that the bear with its greater strength and stamina will ultimately win. I don't have any choice in the matter really but to try and reach the safety of the glacier. So it would be best if I left now while the bear is still occupied tearing my tent to pieces.

It seems to take a lifetime of effort to reach the crest of the ridge overlooking the glacier. But I'm happy now, because below me, just a short snow and ice slope away, lies one of the largest glaciers that I have ever seen, the Main West Fork Glacier. How I have longed to see this great river of ice, just to take in the sheer beauty of it all. The trouble is that I daren't wait around up here for too long, the bear might still be following me, although I can't see any sign of it yet. But it's best if I take no chances.

I reach the safety of the Main West Fork Glacier, after jumping across a deep and frightening crevasse. Two shimmering walls of ice tower up on either side of me now, flanking the glacier, and sparkling in the early morning sunlight. The further I travel up the glacier, the higher they will become, until in a couple of days' time, if I've got my calculations right, Mount Hess will appear.

I can't wait to get started.

I've had a tremendous adventure so far in crossing the wilderness, with enough danger en route to last me a lifetime. Perhaps someone else might decide to turn round here, not wishing to chance his luck any further. However, I came out here to climb Mount Hess, and so long as there are snow caves to shelter in, and food to eat, nothing is going to distract me from my objective.

My journey across the wilderness is complete. Now for the glacier, then the mountain.

Chapter 5

Ice Palace

It's just a small crevasse really, but it bars my route. Yet I still hesitate to jump across. In a way I feel such a fool because it's only the tiniest of splits in the surface of the glacier, and the first of a hundred I'll have to cross if I'm to make any progress at all towards my objective. However, this is my first day on the glacier, so I haven't had time to get used to these obstacles. But even though I know all this, I still hesitate to jump across. The penalty for failure is death. Travelling solo on a glacier concentrates the mind.

I continue to climb directly up the glacier for hour after hour, but it's time I changed course and started heading out more towards a moraine bank located near the centre of the great river of ice. This long ribbon of stones will provide me with a relative safe highway straight up the glacier. The rocks in this medial moraine will have filled in most of the crevasses along my route, but first there are a few kilometres of glacier to cross, full of cunningly concealed holes. This search for hidden crevasses has of necessity to be a calculated economical affair. I couldn't possibly probe every step of the way. Another long narrow split in the ice suddenly obstructs my path, but this time caused by the changing course of the glacier. Fortunately I can see this particular one, so it represents no real problem. It's the crevasses that lie hidden just below a thin surface layer of snow that worry me the most. The upper part of any glacier can be the most troublesome in this respect, although I'm still far too low down for this to be a real concern to me yet.

I soon reach the rocks of the central medial moraine and climb up onto the crest of this high bank of stones. I continue to make fast progress along the top of the moraine bank, heading straight up the glacier now towards the foot of Mount Hess, still some twenty-five kilometres away, around a sharp bend at the head of the glacier. There are twenty hours of daylight to play with here. So it will be my determination to push my route forward that will limit the distance I can cover more than the amount of daylight available.

I'm almost caught by surprise when the sky finally begins to darken. There's not the slightest doubt in my mind that it's night-time now. What can have happened to all those hours that must have passed since I got up this morning? I don't feel in any way tired. My foot feels a lot better now. My encounter with the bear in the ravine hasn't affected me in any serious way. It must be all the excitement of being in amongst the real mountains. Either way, I'm not about to stop now. I must push my route forward at every opportunity, especially during this period of good weather. There'll be plenty of time to sleep later on tonight.

I'm soon forced to stop to clean my misting snow goggles with the corner of a neatly folded handkerchief. When I turn around to look back down the glacier, I can see the trail that I made this morning more clearly now, stretching out all the way behind me. I can't help but wonder if this great trench in the snow is the first one ever made up here by a human being.

The strength of the wind increases, bringing with it an unwelcome change in the weather. As if to emphasize the point, a whole series of light snow flurries begin to roll down the glacier towards me. Most of these hit me square in the face, no matter which way I try to turn my head. I'm going to need some kind of temporary shelter soon in amongst the rocks of the central medial moraine bank to wait out the storm.

The frequency of huge rocks running along the crest of the moraine soon increases and the gaps in between them form natural shelters. It's not long before the entrance to a small cave presents itself. With not the slightest hesitation I pass out of the storm and enter another world.

The silence inside the cave is deafening after the roar of the wind outside, the blackness absolute. The interior is constructed of around thirty of the most perfect square-cut blocks of granite. This cave of mine must surely rival any ancient burial tomb, only it is completely empty. Four stone walls surrounding me, there's a flat stone floor beneath my feet and a roof, covered in low quality quartz crystals, above my head. There's even running water in the form of a constant drip in the corner of the roof of my shelter. This cave would make an ideal base camp from which to climb the mountain, if it were not far too low down on the glacier to be of any real use.

I think I'll leave my water-bottle filling up beneath the long dripping crack while I have something to eat. A single bar of Cadbury's Dairy Milk Chocolate transports me to paradise. Although, upon reflection, I am in that special place already here in the mountains.

I begin to search for my first aid kit, hidden somewhere deep inside my rucksack below candles, matches, gas stove, karabiners – and there it is at last. There's a long cut running down the outside of my left ankle. I can't stop myself from worrying about the possibility of infection if ignored. All meat-eating animals have a degree of rotting meat under their claws. Fortunately, I'm carrying plenty of iodine with me. It should be sufficient to take care of any souvenir from the bear.

My water-bottle hasn't filled up yet. I begin to pace up and down the floor of my cave in my frustration to be away. But there are not going to be many opportunities quite like this one, on a heavily silted glacier, to fill it up with clean drinking water that doesn't require at least a degree of filtering.

I continue to pace, running my fingers along the walls of my shelter as I do so. Then just as I reach a corner, my fingers fall into a vertical crack separating the two huge slabs of granite. The strong white beam of my headtorch first strikes the edges of the crack, then it enters deep inside it. An enormous flash of light rebounds out of the gap between the two walls. I recoil backwards, almost blinded.

The interior of my cave lights up like day. I feel like I'm walking on the inside of a rainbow. This is one of the most incredible sights that I have ever seen. I'm looking end-on at two solid walls of interlocking crystals. I remember a similar discovery I made in the rocks on the Alphubel Glacier high above the village of Tasch in Switzerland. Here I have found two walls that are floor to ceiling of solid crystals, facing in to each other. This glittering mosaic holds me spellbound by its sheer beauty as wave upon wave of rich Alaskan colour pulses in and out of the crack.

My now overflowing water-bottle has become the last thing on my mind. I must try and prise some of the crystals out of the crack. I use the pick of my ice-axe as a lever, and the long tubular shaft of an ice-screw as a fulcrum. Soon I have a magnificent arrangement of violet-coloured crystals in the palm of my left hand. My hand looks like it's on fire now. But I dare not risk snapping the blade of my ice-axe in any further attempts to loosen more crystals. I must stop while I'm ahead. I can always return here at some later date, better equipped and supported, to remove the rest of the crystals. I tuck my modest haul into my rucksack. I'd never be able to carry such a quantity with me anyway. I think, on balance, it would be better if I left my crystal cave intact for another day.

I collect my water-bottle and walk out before I have a chance to change my mind and turn my expedition into a treasure hunt. But I build a large cairn above the entrance to help me to find my crystal cave again.

I've still got a long way to travel today before I'm close enough to my objective to set up a base camp. My foot has improved dramatically. I soon establish a good walking rhythm. I have every intention of getting as far as possible up the glacier, using the smallest amount of energy possible.

I try to break the monotony of testing the trail ahead for crevasses by admiring the scenery around me through what little gaps there are in the mist. It parts to reveal an almost level expanse of ice directly ahead. One of those aircraft that run the now fashionable glacier landing tours could easily land here. The best way to see Alaska is to fly over it, then get in amongst it. You simply turn up at any airfield in the wilderness and off you go. You can fly over one of the three million lakes, or over the gold fields, or just to look down upon the sheer beauty of it all. You name it, and for a reasonable price the pilots will fly you in almost anywhere.

The crevasses start to become more frequent now and one enormous cleft in the ice has completely severed the moraine bank. It extends on both sides of me for as far as I can see through the swirling mist. I quickly remove my snowshoes. I'm going to need my crampons on if I'm to negotiate this great fissure in the ice successfully. I hang my snowshoes around my shoulders. They seem to have found a permanent home there.

I'm going to have to find a suitable snowbridge if I'm to get to the other side safely. Some ten minutes later one comes into view. It looks very fragile, but this is the only one that I can see for hundreds of metres to either side of me. The first steps I take onto the snowbridge are very tentative. But after some soul-searching, I decide to run across it in one go and arrive sweating with fear on the far bank. I know full well that I'm going to have to make many more such crossings if I'm to make any progress towards my mountain.

A small glacier appears out of the mist on the true right bank of the Main West Fork Glacier, entering squarely into the main glacial stream through a chaos of icy boulders. I've always found it tempting to go and explore these tiny sheets of ice and the mountains around them. Of course, the real attraction of these snow-covered peaks is that the routes they contain will have rarely been climbed before. You can almost guarantee that any line you take will be a first ascent. But I can't afford to get side-tracked. I must at all costs stick to my objective for today, that of getting as far as possible up the glacier towards the foot of Mount Hess before establishing a base camp. I wonder whether this is the glacier that connects the Yanert Glacier via a small col to the West Fork. If it is, I'll know for certain just how far I've got to go to reach the foot of Mount

Hess, and I'll be able to orientate myself accurately here on the ground. I sit down on top of a boulder to re-check my map. The trouble is that the weather keeps closing in on me, low clouds in particular obstructing my view of the surrounding mountains. On balance, though, I don't think that this tiny glacier is the one I'm looking for. The ice at the beginning of the slope, for one thing, is far too steep.

I'm suddenly forced into making several wide sweeping detours to avoid a whole series of small lakes sunk deep into the surface of the glacier. The closer I get to them the more brittle the ice seems to become. I walk tentatively around the edge of another exceptionally beautiful heart-shaped stretch of water. My crampons dislodge several large splinters of ice from the rim of the ice cliff surrounding the lake which shower down into the water below. I stop for a moment to watch the ripples spread. But with the ice now starting to crumble around me, I decide to retreat back to safer ground. This is definitely no place to linger.

I must reach another medial moraine bank. My route continues straight up the glacier, but now past a huge rock island, that must be well over six kilometres in length. Once I get close to this island, I'll begin my search for a suitable base camp from which to climb the mountain.

Many exceptionally deep looking crevasses appear ahead of me. It's a wonderful feeling to put my cram-pons back on. At the very least they will give me a feeling of security. But I know full well that wearing them is going to be very tiring on my legs. For this reason I prefer to wear them only on the most difficult and dangerous sections of the glacier.

I crunch my way crisply over the surface. Occasionally a small pebble will catch beneath one of the twelve downward sloping points, only to be sent tiddly-winking across the glacier. It's a great game while it lasts, but the fun has to stop when I reach the final medial moraine bank.

I finish off another delicious bar of Cadbury's Fruit and Nut, sitting high on the very crest of the moraine bank. Then I'm on my way again, walking a little faster this time. The end of my journey for today is in sight. The final leg along the top of the high moraine bank seems to last forever. I start to become very tired indeed. However, from past experience, I know full well that when the ground does finally level off, and I remove my rucksack, all my energy will come flooding back, well, most of it.

I stop walking to listen.

There's a droning noise coming from somewhere lower down on the glacier. It could be an aircraft? The noise suddenly becomes louder. I can definitely see one coming straight up the centre of the glacier towards me. I wonder if the pilot will see me? Although, I'm far too tired now to care if he sees me or not. I watch the aircraft pass directly overhead. I can see the pilot and one passenger sitting behind him in the cockpit. But has anyone seen me? The passenger could have spotted me, but neither of them show the slightest sign that they have seen my lone red-jacketed figure out on the glacier.

The edge of the glacier soon comes into sight. I must leave the moraine bank and start my search for an underground base camp. I'm spoilt for choice really. There are hundreds of deep crevasses to choose from. I should really establish my base camp as far up the glacier towards the foot of Mount Hess as possible. But I'm far too tired to go any further today. I sit down on top of a convenient rock to rest. I lie down. I close my eyes. Then I open them once more. The clouds keep drifting past me in the way they have for most of my journey up the glacier. There's been so little really good visibility to enable me to get an absolutely certain fix on my position that doubts begin to creep in about where I really am. Is this even the Main West Fork Glacier? Or have I taken a wrong turning somewhere? But the doubts now taking place in my mind are born more out of tiredness than anything else. Still I'm going to find out the truth soon if I find myself climbing on the wrong mountain.

I'm drawn towards another beautiful lake sunk deep into the surface of the glacier. Vertical walls of ice curve around it in an almost perfect circle, some several hundred metres in diameter, and nine metres down to the surface of the water in the lake below which reflects an almost perfect mirror image of the surrounding walls of blue green ice back up at me. On the surface float four square-cut icebergs. There's not a single ripple to flaw the picture. Never have I seen a place so tranquil. My journey across the north polar icecap, across half of Alaska, across the great Alaskan wilderness, has now been worthwhile just to see and feel this special moment in time.

My rucksack falls to the ground behind me with a loud thud the moment I release the straps. I lie down on a granite boulder overlooking the lake. The top of this beautiful rock fits me like a glove. There's even a small pedestal of milky white quartz to put my feet on. I lie back, head resting on my climbing helmet, looking straight up the continuing glacier. It leads, like the super highway it is, past the rock island, around a corner in a great sweeping arc to the left, heading straight towards the foot of Mount Hess.

Perhaps if tomorrow I start out climbing as close as possible to the side of this island, which is still the dominant feature of the glacier, I might be able to avoid the worst areas of crevasses. There's nothing worse than getting held up in a great tangle of crevasses at the very beginning of a climb.

I stand up to take a compass bearing in the direction of the island, just in case there's a mist in the morning, and write the six figure reference down on the front cover of my map. I lay my map and compass down beside me. I'll put them both away later on.

It's relaxing to lie back on top of my warm rock once more, looking down upon the dancing surface of the lake. I have made the deliberate choice as a climber of having no details of my route up the mountain. I feel like an adventurer. This is what it must have been like in the beginning, for the early pioneers of the climbing world.

Jesus Christ! The water really is dancing around on the surface of the lake. It is covered in a thousand tiny moving pinnacles. I continue to look down in sheer amazement. What on earth is happening? Then it just seems to explode. Thousands of tiny water droplets suddenly jump high into the air. Then it goes super calm once more. But it's not long before the pinnacles of water return to dance before me. It's almost as if the lake is being shaken by some gigantic unseen hand. The pinnacles of water begin to grow larger once more.

The answer to what's happening is only moments away. A solid wall of snow suddenly explodes into view, rolling straight down the glacier towards me. I jump down off my boulder in sheer fright and only just manage to get my head down behind the rock before the leading edge of the avalanche reaches me. My ice-axe is still in my right hand. I quickly drive the shaft deep into a crack in the ice beside me. The snow begins to scream over the top of my head now, thrown up into the air by the smooth upward curvature of the granite boulder sheltering me. The suction from the avalanche tears at the clothing on my back. I grip the shaft of my ice-axe even tighter. Everything goes black in a screaming hell of wind-blown snow and blocks of ice tearing past low over the top of my head. Then another really big blast of snow hits the front of the rock sheltering me. I can feel snow being forced down the back of my neck and into every opening in my clothing.

The avalanche suddenly stops. Fortunately the main thrust of the debris passed well over to one side of me. I burst out from beneath the snow. It is knee-deep all around me now, and starting to set like concrete. There's a calm wind blowing high overhead and a clear blue sky. It's almost as if nothing has happened here at all. But the landscape now bears witness to what has taken place. There's a new stream flowing where before there was none, gouged out of the glacier by hundreds of huge boulders to form a shallow channel that is still filling up with water. The glacier around me has changed out of all recognition, but it's still the one that I'll have to climb tomorrow morning, new layer of avalanche snow or not. I'm convinced now more than ever before of the wisdom of selecting an underground base camp, safe from avalanches.

I clearly remember laying my map and compass down on the rock just before the avalanche struck. What a stupid mistake to have made. I should have put them both away the moment I'd finished using them. I'll not see either of them again. I can only count myself lucky in that I've committed a great deal of the basic detail of my route up the mountain to memory.

I must look for a shelter now. There are an enormous number of holes in the glacier to choose from. But which one do I use for a base camp? I shine my headtorch down inside the nearest crevasse. The strong white beam of light soon breathes life into the darkness. There's nothing but empty space inside this one. There's no bottom to it either that I can see. It looks like I'm going to have to try the next crevasse in the row. There's only the tiniest of holes to be seen on the surface of the glacier. I soon widen it with the pick of my ice-axe. Then I lie down flat on my stomach and look down into the hole. There's a gently sloping ramp of rocks to tempt me down.

My boots hit the floor of the ramp with a loud crash of slithering pebbles. There's the thrill of the unknown lurking here. My headtorch lights the way between two enormous vertical walls of blue ice. My pulse begins to race with the excitement of breaking new ground. What lies at the bottom of my deep underground passage? I can only just make out the beginnings of a large chamber, just a short distance ahead of me now, at the bottom of the slope. This must surely be the base camp I've been seeking.

The ice chamber at the bottom of the ramp is enormous. There's another short tunnel, big enough to stand up in, in the far wall, which leads me round a tight corner, through a hole into a straight and pencil-like tunnel. One end is blocked by a pile of boulders. I walk very carefully back in the opposite direction. I think I'll call this the long watercourse tunnel, because that is what it must once have been. The long water-course tunnel ends abruptly in another hole halfway up a wall of ice surrounding a magnificent lake sunk deep into the surface of the glacier. This must surely be the same lake that I was looking at just before the ava-lanche struck. The icebergs floating around in it are definitely the same ones. A powerful stream has definitely sculptured the long watercourse tunnel, with the water having been diverted elsewhere, most probably by the same avalanche of rocks that is now blocking up the far end of the tunnel. The sun blisters down upon me as I stand in the oval-shaped tunnel exit high above the lake. A shimmering white heat haze is reflecting up at me from the mirror surface of the water below and down upon me from the snow and ice on the glacier above. It's tempting to linger, soaking up the sun, but there are important things to be done back inside my shelter.

I walk very carefully back along the bed of the watercourse tunnel, climb up through the hole in the wall, back through the short curving tunnel into my large underground sleeping chamber. There's my evening meal to cook now. Then there's my bivouac to prepare. I must get this place looking more like home.

I assemble a large quantity of rocks from the sloping floor of the ramp to insulate me from the cold. I lay the rocks evenly over the floor of my shelter, in true block-paving fashion. A fine dusting of smaller pebbles fills in the gaps between the rocks, and finishes off the floor of my sleeping chamber. My bivouac is ready now with my sleeping bag laid out neatly on top of my karrimat. There are even two small red candles, each burning brightly in separate alcoves, on opposite walls of my shelter. I have a roof over my head now and a clean water supply down by the lake.

This is my ideal base camp from which to climb the mountain, and good enough to be called the Ice Palace.

I hardly dare believe my luck at finding such a natural shelter instead of the usual bleak and inhospitable crevasse. I have a ready-made fully furnished apartment, no rent or water rates to pay, swimming pool out back, even regular avalanches above to keep the tourists at bay, and all ideally situated some 295 kilometres north-north-east of Anchorage.

I must get a rope handrail fixed in place on the walls of the various tunnels, just in case I get caught out in one of them in the dark. I tie my rope to a boulder out on the glacier, then lower it down through the hole. At a point approximately halfway down the entrance ramp I secure it to an ice-screw driven deep into the right-hand wall of ice. I thread the rest of my rope down through my sleeping chamber, through the short curving tunnel, then down through the lower section of the long water-course tunnel and out through the hole in the wall high above the lake. The noise of all my hammering still echoes loudly in my ears as I drive in several more ice-screws. My complete rope is in place now, all 147 metres of it, the last few centimetres dangling down into the water in the lake below, with my water-bottle tied onto the end.

Bubbling, gurgling and popping, in a blaze of brilliant white sunlight, it soon fills and I haul it up through the hole in the wall and pour the contents into a large cooking pan. As I refill my water-bottle, I think about the delicious meat and vegetable stew that I'm going to make once I get my pan full of water safely back inside my sleeping chamber. But I'm going to need all the patience and balance of a tightrope walker first not to spill any. I've never yet succeeded in returning to a bivouac without some spillage which of course means having to go back and start all over again. Half a pan of water is never enough. Holding an ice-cold pan, even with gloves, doesn't help matters either. I pass my pan from hand to hand in a desperate attempt to keep my fingers from freezing. It's a great relief to lay it down on the floor of the short curving tunnel and climb in after it, before taking the last few steps along the dish-shaped floor into my sleeping chamber. I soon have my pan of water boiling on top of my gas stove. I can't help but smile at my success. I've always known that I would eventually succeed on one of my expeditions to Alaska in collecting a pan full of water and transporting it all the way back to my bivouac without spilling a single drop, and I've done it, here inside the Ice Palace, on my way to climb Mount Hess.

There's just one last task to perform before I go to sleep. I must build three cairns in a straight line out on the glacier before the weather closes in on me completely. These piles of stones will, in the absence of my map and compass, help to point me in the right direction when it's time to leave here early tomorrow morning. It's hot work building the cairns, even on a glacier now covered in long shadows, but soon all three are in place. At least I can be sure of starting out in the right direction tomorrow. I'm not too bothered now if the weather does close in on me. A freezing cold mist has already descended over the area, and I shiver as I sit on the edge of my entrance hole having one last look around before descending the ramp to the relative warmth below.

Chapter 6

Ice Tomb

I can't think why I have decided to sit here on the edge of the entrance hole at this precise moment, looking at what little scenery there is to be seen through the gaps in the mist. Maybe some unseen hand is offering me that one last sensation of life-giving fresh air in the real above-ground world before allowing fate to run its course?

Why should I bother to use my rope handrail? It has already started to become familiar to me. Of course familiarity breeds contempt, a state of mind that gives rise to a false belief that you know all the answers, that you are invulnerable. It's in this last belief that I am sadly mistaken. Only one error of judgement is required when climbing to bring about a complete and utter disaster.

Suddenly I find myself landing with a crash of moving rocks on the sloping floor of the ramp. I hold my hands out on either side of me to steady myself down through the darkness. The heels on my heavy climbing boots are tending to create their own steps in the loose scree, each time I step down the slope. There's only the noisy echo of slithering pebbles to be heard around me now. Then without any warning at all, I plunge down into a hole in the floor of the ramp and come to a sudden violent stop. A nauseating feeling sweeps over me. I'm jammed up to my chest in the hole, with my left arm pinned tightly to my side, my legs dangling over God knows how great a void. Only my head and shoulders and right arm are left sticking up through the floor.

There's only a single shaft of light filtering down from somewhere high above me now on the surface of the glacier, left to illuminate my plight and the settling dust storm all around me. The perilous nature of my situation is all too obvious to me. I'm stuck in a hole in the sloping floor of the ramp, with an enormous amount of rubble on the slope above me, mostly loose rocks and gravel, all waiting to come sliding down to engulf me. The only thing preventing this is my own body plugging the hole. I'm literally holding the slope up. If I make the slightest move to free myself the debris will come sliding down towards me. I'm caught in the most terrible trap imaginable. The weight of the boulders on the slope above me is already starting to squeeze the life out of me, making it very difficult for me to breathe. And if they don't succeed, the crevasse wall of clear blue ice will freeze the life out of me. I've got to act to save myself now. If I don't make a move I'm going to lose all movement in my arms and legs. I must try to free myself, regardless of the consequences.

I've got to free my left arm first. I'm going to need both of them to shift the debris in front of me. But it's no use. I can't move my left arm at all. I can't seem to get any kind of purchase on the wall of the crevasse behind me with my climbing boots either. I twist and turn. If only I could somehow get the heels on my climbing boots to stay fixed on the wall of the crevasse behind me, then I would be able to thrust myself up out of the hole. But my boots, good as they are for most types of climbing, just keep sliding down off the ice. It's no use, I'm never going to succeed here.

However, I'm sure I can feel the pressure beginning to ease in the area around my chest. Something is definitely on the move. There's the distinct smell of sulphur in the air, too. It's strange but I haven't noticed this all-pervading odour before. It has obviously come from some of the many collisions that must have taken place between the rocks when the floor of the ramp collapsed. However the sharp smell of sulphur is the last thing on my mind now. Rocks are on the move once more. Only this time they are not moving from around the area of my chest, instead they begin to slide down the slope towards me from somewhere high above.

I watch horrified as the first few tiny pebbles come bouncing down the slope, spinning in front of my face, before continuing on down the slope, and into my sleeping chamber. More follow, then smaller grains of

95

sand start to trickle down the slope like so many deadly rivers of death. This debris starts to pile up against the sides of my face. I'm going to be buried by it sooner or later. I lift my right arm and I place it in front of my face. I must try to divert the sand away from me. I must at all costs protect my face. I close my eyes. I try to shut out the nightmare. But I can't block it out.

The rising tide of rocks, sand and gravel begins to creep up around the sides of my face now. It doesn't seem to matter how much debris I remove, more takes its place. It is already dangerously close to covering my nose and mouth completely. I must act to save myself. I'm slowly being suffocated. I can hardly breathe at all now. I start to panic. I scoop the sand away from my mouth. But for every handful I remove, another replaces it. I can't hold my breath much longer. I begin to scream out loud. "Will someone help me?" But of course there is no one out here to come to my aid. My legs feel lifeless below me. My lips have lost all feeling. I continue to claw at the debris in front of my face with my one free hand. My lungs must be close to bursting. My fingers suddenly push through into my mouth and air rushes in. I can breathe once more. But the battle isn't over yet.

It seems to take an age to remove all the sand and gravel from around the sides of my face. I open my eyes. The debris on the slope above me has stopped moving now. I spit the remaining fine grains of sand out of my mouth. I even manage to blow my nose. It still tickles. I press my left nostril tight up against the sleeve of my red down jacket. A single ray of bright sunlight momentarily illuminates my arm. I turn my head around to look upwards. There's still the same ray of light shining down from somewhere high above on the surface. I twist my head around even further now, encouraged by the light, trying to see as far as possible up the sloping floor of the ramp. But there's still nothing but dusty darkness. The harsh reality of my situation is that I'm still trapped and being held more tightly than before.

The ice around me starts to moan.

I'm sure I can hear groaning noises coming from deep within the heart of the glacier. Then more start up in the ice all around me. These noises begin to sound like voices now, with one half of the glacier seeming to talk to the other, and mocking the folly of a man who presumed to be safe within it, who dared to try alone and failed. Or are these noises within the glacier all in my mind? I'm sure my imagination is playing tricks on me. My sleeping chamber, only a short distance below me, is in total darkness. The candles there must have been blown out, or blown over, by the blast of air from the avalanche of rocks when the floor of the ramp collapsed. Thank goodness for the single ray of light shining down from above. At the very least it gives me some hope that I might be able to get out of here alive. It seems to turn many colours now. Who knows why the light has done this, but they are beautiful in every way.

And the time passes by, time for my red down jacket to slide, ever so slowly, up around my chest, as I begin to sink further down inside the hole. The very idea that this could be happening almost throws me into a panic. This gradual downward movement was hardly noticeable at first. But I can definitely feel myself sliding now. What will happen to me if I fall all the way through the floor of the ramp? I suppose that the rocks above me will immediately roll down the slope to seal me up inside my tomb.

Who is going to rescue me now? There is no one out here to save me. John knows I'll be climbing up the Main West Fork Glacier at some point in the expedition. What he doesn't know, is that I'm trapped under it. The only way that I'm ever going to get out of here is if I attempt to rescue myself. I've got to make a move now while I've still got the strength left to do so. The first thing that I must do, if I can't free my left arm, is try and reach my rope handrail, still out of sight, somewhere high above my head. I can only hope that my rope is still there.

If only I could somehow turn my head around and look for my rope handrail. But I can't do that. I'm facing in the wrong direction. But I've got to believe that it is still there, fixed to the wall of the crevasse behind me, the same one that is now trying to freeze the life out of me. The trouble is that every time I try to turn my head around to look upwards more rubble begins to move down the slope towards me, forcing me to turn around and stop. Regardless of this, I reach blindly high above my head with my right hand. But each time all I feel is icy wall. It's no use, I've got to rest now. I must save all my remaining energy for one really good try later on. I allow my arm to fall forward, on top of the rubble in front of me. I'll try again, later on . . .

A film of ice has started to form on my clothing, soaked through by the constant contact with the dripping wall of the crevasse behind me. The cold is intense now. It threatens to freeze the very muscles in my arms and legs needed to help me escape. I make one more convulsive effort. But I'm sure that I can feel something. It comes as a shock to find that I can feel anything at all. I'm suddenly sparked into life. I lunge upwards once more. My fingers close around my rope. I have it firmly in my grasp now. But with my right arm now stretched to the very limit of my long reach, high above my head, I seem to have become smaller in the area around my chest, and I begin to slide further down inside the hole in the sloping floor of the ramp. My shoulders are almost level with the slope itself now. I've got to let go of my rope if I'm to expand my chest and stop this gradual downward movement. But if I do that, then I'll never be able to pull myself up out of the hole. I simple dare not let go of my rope now. Whatever I do I must keep calm. I've only got one chance left.

I must put everything that I've got into a single pull that will take me up out of the hole. I'm never going to have the strength left to do it twice, not after all my previous attempts to drag myself clear. I'm never going to let go of my rope, no matter what the consequences. My arms have never been my strongest point. Every day I've lifted weights in a determined effort to build up my biceps. Perhaps I've waited all my life for this one single moment to prove it was all worth while. I can feel the tension in the air around me. I must put everything that I've got into a single move to pull myself up out of the hole. I've got to succeed. I'm never going to have another chance of escaping. The fingers on my right hand are still locked tightly around my rope. I'm as ready as I ever will be.

I gradually lift myself, twisting, turning and kicking, slowly up out of the hole, until my chest clears the sharp rocks on the floor of the ramp. I push myself forward onto the rubble in front of me, with my boots only just managing to stay in place on the wall of the crevasse behind me. I want to shout out for joy. But I'm never going to maintain this new position. I can feel myself slowly begin to slide backwards into the hole once more. There's absolutely nothing that I can do to prevent this from happening. My weight is proving to be too great for the natural stretch of the rope. It is never going to take my full weight without stretching to a certain degree. I gradually sink back into the hole. My rope suddenly comes tight in my hand once more. I'm back where I started. I feel devastated.

A sense of utter despair sweeps over me. I begin to panic. What more can I do? Surely I've done enough? Everything has been against me on this expedition. This time, stuck in a hole in the sloping floor of the ramp, my best just has not been good enough. There are some situations that can never be won. But I'm never going to let go of my rope. I may have lost the battle. But I haven't lost my determination to hold onto my rope. I'm finished now. Perhaps someone will find my body twenty years from now with my right hand still locked tight onto my rope in a last defiant gesture to the world. Then again, perhaps no one will ever locate me so deep under the ice on such an enormous glacier. I've got nothing to lose now. I'll twist and turn as much as I want to. I'll bring the whole fucking glacier down upon my head if I have to. It's surprising what reserves of strength one can find in an emergency.

I twist my complete body around to the left. Then just as violently I turn to the right, in a superhuman effort to free my left arm. And suddenly it comes free. The glass covering the face of my wrist-watch shatters, but with my arms free at last, and using them both to pull on the rope, I lift myself clear of the hole. I throw myself forward on top of the debris in front of me once more, pushing my boots hard into the wall of ice behind. Then I let go of my rope before it has a chance to stretch any further and lower me back down inside the hole. The boulders high on the slope above me are already beginning to move down towards me. I must get out of here. I dig my fingers deep into the loose gravel on the floor of the ramp. I pull myself forward. My legs come free of the hole. I quickly regain my feet. I stagger forward down the lower half of the ramp. I turn the corner into my sleeping chamber. I lie down on top of my sleeping bag. It's a long time before the noise of falling rocks subsides.

I'm not sure what to do now for the best. I could always abandon my expedition and retrace my steps back to the Denali Highway. Or should I carry on with my original plans to climb Mount Hess? I could, of course, simply stay here, in the area of the Ice Palace. This part of the glacier is as good a place as any to spend the rest of my vacation. I could get up early tomorrow morning and go for a swim in the lake outside. I could even go sunbathing, although doing those things on a glacier are never a good idea. I could of course, simply go to sleep right now and let tomorrow take care of itself. Anyway I simply don't have the necessary food to stay here any longer than a few days. So I can't afford to spend a single one in idleness. I should really have planned to have had about two weeks' supply of food with me at this point in the expedition, not the mere four days' that I have left. But I'm the one that's having to carry it, no one else is going to do it for me. I said no to air drops. For me here there are just endless Alaskan days and nights of effort, and they are not going to be wasted.

If I am to get a fast start early tomorrow morning, I must get what's left of my rope fixed to the wall of ice surrounding the lake outside as soon as possible. This is the only way out of the Ice Palace now. I must get my rope in place while I've still got the energy and enthusiasm left to do so. The ramp is completely blocked up with debris. I'm never going to be able to get out that way again. But I must salvage as much of my rope as possible from within the lower half of the ramp. I don't like the idea of having to enter that dangerous area at all, but I'm going to need every bit of rope that I can salvage if I'm going to climb out of here. I pull on the end of my rope, from the safety of my sleeping chamber, but it is still firmly embedded in the rocks blocking the top half of the ramp. I'm left with no choice but to cut it, as close to the blockage as I dare go. But I've still got enough rope left to climb on.

I walk back through my sleeping chamber, coiling my rope handrail in as I go. Then I remove it from the wall of the short curving tunnel. I walk through the long watercourse tunnel, still coiling my rope into great big loops, all the way down to the edge of the hole in the wall surrounding the lake.

The light reflected up from the surface of the water and down from the glacier seems very bright after spending so much time in total darkness. But I enjoy the splendid sight of the moonlit icebergs floating about on the surface of the lake, still held captive within the walls of blue-green ice.

There's the usual desperate scramble to get the picks on my axes securely placed on the surface of the glacier after climbing to the top of the wall of ice surrounding the lake. Unfortunately one of my karabiners slips from my cold fingers and lands with a loud splash in the water. I could easily follow it down into the lake if I'm not too careful. The night-time temperature of the water must be cold enough to give anyone a heart attack. The sooner I'm off this wall of rotten ice and standing safely on the glacier the better. I reach up once

more and, grasping the pick on my most secure axe
with both my hands this time, I finally pull myself up
over the edge and onto level ground. I lie back in the
snow, looking up at the patchy clouds. I'm far too tired
to even think about standing up. I remain lying down
for some time. Perhaps I'll remain here forever. The
night sky looks so beautiful above me, the moon's glow
so soothing on my face. If I had fallen off the wall of ice I
would have been finished. Perhaps it's time I gave up
climbing, and took on a more gentle pastime, although,
I doubt if I could ever do that. Climbing is far too
beautiful an experience.

I tie my rope around a boulder close to the edge of
the ice wall surrounding the lake. Then I lower it down
to the hole in the wall. I can abseil down to the
entrance leading into my shelter whenever I want to
now.

I'm sure I heard voices? Are there climbers on the
glacier? I turn around to scan its length and breadth for
as far as I can see through the mist that has suddenly
returned. So far I haven't come across a trace of any
other climbers operating in the area. But if there are
other people on the glacier calling out, they could be
lost in the mist. I ought to try and help. Also they could
have some spare food with them. I continue to peer
hard into the now lightly falling snowflakes, but the
harsh reality is that I'm far too tired to begin a
systematic search of the area. Yet I can't go back inside
my shelter without at least making some attempt at
contact.

ICE TOMB

"Is anyone out there?"

There's still no reply at all to my loud shouts . . . until a loud grunting noise comes drifting back to me from somewhere far out across the other side of the glacier, then several more similar noises.

The sound of a creature grunting is the one thing I definitely don't want to be hearing at this moment. I want to be listening to human voices. I'm still not absolutely certain that these strange sounds are grunting noises. Only one thing's for certain, I'm not going to wait around here to find out the truth. I must get back inside my shelter as quickly as possible. I'm suddenly filled with a terrible fear. I never thought, even in my wildest dreams, that I would be happy to be back inside such a dangerous place as the Ice Palace. But if there is a bear roaming about on the glacier, then my shelter must be the safest place around. I quickly abscil down to the hole in the wall. I swing back inside the long watercourse tunnel. At least I can be reasonably sure now that no bear will be able to reach me, since the only other entrance, on the glacier, is blocked up with boulders.

I find myself laughing out loud in an almost uncontrollable manner as I walk back through the long watercourse tunnel into my sleeping chamber. But my laughter is not that of someone having a ball. Instead, it's the nervous faltering laugh of someone desperately trying to convince himself that bears do not venture out onto glaciers.

I soon pack my equipment away. Then I eat a simple

vegetable soup. I'm ready for the climb on Mount Hess tomorrow. I've got four days' supply of food left, three days' rations to go with me tomorrow and a single day's supply to be left here inside the Ice Palace, ready for my return, cached inside one of the alcoves containing one of my red candles. I snuggle down deeper inside my sleeping bag. I'll leave my candles to burn themselves out.

My rucksack is packed. My food is securely tied to the top in a green canvas kitbag. The rest of my equipment is laid out neatly on the floor of my sleeping chamber ready for tomorrow. All I have to do is climb up my fixed rope above the lake, then walk some fourteen kilometres up the glacier to the start of the real climbing on the mountain itself. The last part of my journey is a great curving arc to the left, around a sharp bend at the head of the glacier, below the huge South-West Ridge of Mount Hess. The lower half of this long ridge should contain a col, if my memory serves me right. I've no way of checking this any longer, of course. But if there is a col on the South-West Ridge of Mount Hess, I'll spend the night up there, hoping I can simply dig into a suitable bank of snow.

The next day I plan to climb the ridge all the way to the summit of Mount Hess. It remains to be seen if my plan will work in practice. I'm under no illusions as to the serious nature of the climbing to be done tomorrow, but a ridge is a ridge. I soon fall into a deep sleep, far too tired to care whether the black shadow of a bear might be creeping up over the lake outside.

Chapter 7

The Climb

The ice above me radiates an eerie sort of glow, a luminescence suggesting warmth, yet only the cold reaches me. I secure every possible zip, button and draw-cord against the cold. Then I pull the straps of my climbing helmet tight under my chin. I step into my sit-harness, both jumar clamps already attached, ready to be clipped onto the waiting rope outside.

The all too familiar clang of ice-screws and karabiners accompanies me as I walk along the tunnel towards the exit high above the lake. How many climbs have started this way, walking through a long cold dark tunnel, carved out of the ice: the tunnel leading out onto the Jungfraufirn from the Jungfraujoch railway station in Switzerland, for climbs on the Eiger, Mönch and Jungfrau; the Midi cableway station in France, leading out onto the Midi Plan Ridge. Each has its own individual character and fascination, but all have one thing in common, they guide you out into a world of incredible beauty.

I soon jumar up my rope heading for the top of the ice cliff. I haven't forgotten the strange grunting noises that I heard on the glacier yesterday. Yet there's nothing to be seen or heard of any bear. The mist is bound to hide me anyway, even if there is one up here. After coiling my rope around my shoulders, I stride purposefully forward. There are some really good snow conditions underfoot that will enable me to make fast progress towards the foot of Mount Hess.

The remainder of the Main West Fork Glacier goes remarkably incident free. There's just the odd ava-lanche to be heard thundering down on either side of me from the walls bordering the glacier. This keeps me on my toes, but really it's just a case of keeping my head down and making sure but steady progress over pleasant snow and ice conditions, turning the occa-sional crevasse where necessary.

The glacier suddenly steepens considerably, but it's not long before it levels out once more. Then it turns sharply to the left below the huge South-West Ridge of Mount Hess.

I begin a great curving traverse below the ridge, keeping as close to the crevasse (the bergschrund) separating the glacier from the flank of the ridge itself as I possibly can. I feel a lot safer climbing well over to one side of the glacier.

I'm still hoping to climb up to a small col, somewhere in the lower half of the ridge, just south of the secondary summit and bivouac there before my summit push. The timing of this will be difficult to achieve without knowing the correct time. My wrist-watch was broken back at the Ice Palace. Watch or no watch, however, it comes down to the basic fact that if the snow is frozen solid, then I go, if it is soft, then I wait.

I arrive gasping for breath just below the bergschrund and scramble across the only snowbridge that I can see for hundreds of metres on either side of me. It's a great relief to have negotiated this successfully and I start to climb the steep ice slope that will, I hope, lead me onto the col. A mixed snow and ice slope faces me, crumpled in places, the occasional rock island jutting out from beneath the snow. It is bordered on either side by a narrow ridge.

It comes as rather a shock to be moving upwards after spending so many hours contouring the glacier. But I'm glad to be on the mountain proper at last. I continue to zigzag up the steep ice slope for hour after hour. I gradually enter a freezing belt of cloud. Moisture on my clothing freezes into a thin transparent layer of ice that crackles and splinters with every movement that I make. Icicles begin to grow on each individual hair hanging down from beneath the front of my climbing helmet.

When I finally burst through the clouds it is into the most dazzling display of light I have ever seen. I must stop to soak up the sun. The glare from the sun is intense. I quickly pull my snow-goggles down over my eyes. The sun continues to blister down upon me. I can't resist its power. I turn to face it. Burn me till I'm brown. Burn me to a crisp sun.

THE CLIMB

An enormous layer of cloud stetches out before me under a shimmering white heat haze that seems to stretch all the way back to the Gulf of Alaska and beyond. Row upon row of mountain tops stick up through this fluffy white layer of clouds, like so many tiny island havens in a storm. Above them all, Mount Hess stands tall, flanked on either side by Mount Deborah and Mount Hayes. Together they seem to be standing guard over Alaska's northern slope. All the words ever written and spoken about these mountains are true. Mount Hess in particular looks very impressive.

It's not long before I'm stopped by an exceptionally wide crevasse. I'm going to have to climb down inside it to a point where it narrows down at the bottom then climb up the opposite wall. It is very difficult if not impossible to successfully jump a crevasse on the up-slope and this one is too wide anyway.

I quickly straddle across between the two freezing walls of ice, stretching myself to the very limit of my stride. Then I spring across the gap onto the far wall of the crevasse, with the front-points on my crampons and the picks on both my axes holding me securely in place. I wish my rucksack was not weighing me down. Handicapped though I am, I make a very determined effort to climb the opposite wall of the crevasse, with my crampons scrambling and scraping to get a good purchase. If I fall off, I will surely die, for I haven't secured myself in order to save time. You can't secure every move on a mountain. Yet I love every wonderful

moment of the struggle. It is everything to me. This is
the stuff that climbing dreams are made of. It's not long
before I stand, somewhat exhausted, and a little out of
breath, but happy, on the opposite side of the crevasse
and move off up the steep ice slope once more, into the
next maze of crevasses. The reality here is that no
climber alone on a big mountain route has the time to
get entangled with any serious obstacles like crevasses,
but sometimes these nightmarish systems are unavoid-
able. This time I manage to jump each one in turn as it
appears on the slope above me. I begin to feel like an
Olympic hurdler now, only my attempts are somewhat
handicapped by the weight of my rucksack.

A whole series of crumbling towers of ice appears in
front of me. Falling debris is everywhere. An icy cold
chill passes down through my body as I squeeze between two vertical walls of ice, probing for crevasses
every step of the way. This narrow corridor of ice is the
only way forward now, so it's just as well there are no
big crevasses along this particular passage. And then I
am out into the full glare of the sun once more.
Numerous sun-scorched zigzags follow on behind me
as I continue climbing up the steep ice slope.

The ridge creeps up on me almost unnoticed. It's
only the fact that I've suddenly entered into the enormous shadow of numerous overhanging cornices that
forces me to look up. I must have been concentrating
very hard on climbing the steep ice slope, as one must
in order to stay alive. I can only count myself lucky that
I've ended up directly below a very definite dip in the

ridge, which I assume is the small col. However my way is barred by an almost continuous barrier of overhanging cornices, with only one exception, the area around a high rock step in the ridge just a short distance above me. These great overhanging masses of unstable snow extend in both directions along the ridge for as far as I can see. Any one of these cornices could conceivably collapse under its own weight at any moment. I haven't got a moment to lose here. The sooner I tunnel through the cornice and onto the col the better.

I cut a large step into the slope, as a first priority, as close to the underside of the huge overhanging lip of the cornice as possible. I'm going to need something to stand on until I can get my tunnel started. Once I've tunnelled through the cornice onto the col I'll begin my search for a suitable bank of snow in which to construct my shelter.

I hang my rucksack from the head of my ice-axe pressed hard into the snow beside me. Then I remove my snow-shovel from the side of my rucksack. I'm glad that I decided to keep it now. I've lost track of the number of times that I've wanted to throw it away when it was catching on the tree branches in the cottonwoods and upon the long slim branches sticking out from all the fissures in the wall of the ravine. But using the sharp blade to great effect, I quickly tunnel deep into the heart of the cornice. It's hot work digging, but I persevere, burrow deep and discard each shovel full of snow carefully behind me.

There's a surprising amount of light reaching me

inside my tunnel. I can see everything that needs to be seen. The defused glow of light becomes brighter as my arms begin to ache. However I'm not ready to give up yet. I begin to dig more furiously. I can sense that the end of the tunnel is in sight. Several more powerful thrusts later I break out of the other side of the cornice and into the full glare of the sun.

I crawl forward on my hands and knees. I drop my snow-shovel. I slide, almost out of control now, down the last few metres of steep ice onto the wide open slopes of the col. Tears form in my eyes. I've got to admit the truth to myself. If the col hadn't appeared when it did I could have ended up being buried alive. There's a narrow line in climbing. Once it is crossed, you are totally committed. It becomes a matter of life and death. I have just crossed that narrow line in tunnelling through the heart of the cornice. I have succeeded and, as ever, to the victor go the spoils. In this case it's the summit of Mount Hess.

The weather is quite reasonable at the moment. I should be able to get to the summit and back within a single day tomorrow if the weather stays good.

By the time I've retrieved my rucksack from the start of the tunnel the wind has already begun to scream over the wide open slopes of the col. I'm fortunate here in that I've stumbled across a bank of snow deep enough to contain my shelter. The wind continues to scream past just a short distance above my head, funnelled upwards by the smooth upward curvature of the slopes.

I love to spend as much time as possible, when constructing a shelter, trying to make the perfect home. But this time I'm forced into hurrying just in case the wind alters course. Fortunately, the snow is a perfect consistency for excavating a snow cave, indeed the conditions on the col couldn't be better. It's not long before I have two large platforms (one for sleeping on, the other for my equipment) constructed in the area of warm rising air, high on each wall of a T-shaped shelter.

It's thirsty work digging. A long cool drink of slightly sweetened orange juice, warmed up on top of my gas stove, leaves me feeling refreshed and ready for the final task of shaping the interior walls, using my snow saw this time. It's not long before the sides of my shelter are smoothed down to perfection, making them drip-free. (Bending the blade of my snow saw greatly helps me in doing this.) My clothing should remain dry now, although the normal condensation, from breathing, cooking, etc, will over a period of a few days gradually work its way into all my clothing.

I must cut some snow bricks ready to seal up the entrance to my shelter now. I continue this tedious but necessary task of trimming each block to fit those above and below it precisely and lay the remaining snow bricks down just inside the short entrance tunnel. I've left a small gap just big enough to crawl through. But I'm free to seal it up whenever I like.

I wonder what the weather is going to be like for my summit bid tomorrow? I must have asked myself this same question a hundred times during the past few hours. High lines of cirrus clouds, fine particles of ice in reality, are already approaching my position from over the Gulf of Alaska. These delicate wispy clouds usually herald a change in the weather and, knowing my luck, this is bound to be a change for the worse. Still, I'm not too worried if the weather does go against me. It only needs to hold off for the duration of my summit bid, after that it can do what it likes. Mountains have a habit of creating their own individual weather conditions around themselves, independent of the overall picture. Only time will tell if my prediction of a storm is correct.

I'm in no great hurry to seal myself up inside my shelter. A long cool drink of orange juice taken straight from my water-bottle is what's needed here. Then I lie back on my warm rock, soaking up as much sun as possible. I close my eyes against the full glare and snuggle down deeper inside the hood of my red down jacket. There are only two sounds of any note to be heard now; one is the super cool orange juice pouring down my throat; the other is the wind tearing past just a short distance above my head. I could lie here all day like this. I stretch my arms high above my head in utter contentment.

When I eventually stand up to admire the magnificent view, I pick out the great glacier basin at my feet, with the southernmost slopes of Mount Deborah and the South-West Ridge of Mount Hess bordering the area. On the other side of my somewhat indistinct col, there's another great glacier basin, containing the head, (or névé) of the Main West Fork Glacier itself, directly below the southern rock face of Mount Hess. The tracks that I made in the snow this morning are clearly visible, coming up the Main West Fork Glacier. They cut a neat little groove in the snow as the glacier turns in a great sweeping arc to the left. My trail weaves in and out of the worst areas of crevasses close to the bergschrund. I'm quite proud of my route up the glacier, winding its way around the huge columns of ice, the crevasses, the humps, the hollows.

And then I see something else. There's definitely some creature moving along my trail up the glacier! Good God! Surely it can't be Scar Face? My worst fears are soon confirmed. I can clearly see by the very size of this creature that it's not another human being. I close my eyes. I try to blot out the sight of the great bear. But I'm soon forced to open them. Fear forces me to look. The bear is still there 1300 metres below me, close to the bend in the glacier. It seems to have grown in stature in the space of a few minutes, and very single-minded in its efforts to close the gap between us.

I tell myself that even if it does manage to reach the bottom of the steep ice slope, it will never be able to cross the bergschrund. There's only one snowbridge across this huge crevasse and it is bound to collapse under the weight of such an enormous creature. That simple fact, more than any other, makes me feel a great deal safer. I can only hope that the storm I have predicted will come early. I should be able to hide myself in the clouds. I never thought that I'd be high on a mountain ridge in Alaska praying for a storm to come.

The final snow brick fits neatly into place. The entrance to my shelter is completely blocked up now. There are just two small candle flames left to keep me company while I make a cup of coffee. I've only got a single sachet of coffee left now, hidden away some-where inside my rucksack. I've been saving this for a special occasion – and what could be more special than being high on the South West Ridge of Mount Hess in Alaska. The rich aroma of coffee soon forces its way into every corner of my shelter. If I can no longer stretch out on my warm rock in the sun, I can think of no better sensation than cupping my hands around a steaming hot cup of coffee. The only problem here is that I seem to have an enormous headache to offset this wonderful feeling of warmth. My gas stove must be using up all the oxygen inside my shelter, effectively competing with me for it. I quickly reach out for one of the long ski sticks with which I've been probing for crevasses, and push the pointed end up through the roof of my shelter. My headache clears up almost immediately. What a dif-ference a little ventilation makes. Even my candles seem to be burning brighter. I think I'll leave it where it is, sticking up through the roof of my shelter. A quick wiggle with the end of my ski stick every now and again is all that's going to be needed to keep me breathing throughout the night.

I begin to feel very tired indeed. But there's nothing else that I need to do now except go to sleep, and I must do this as soon as possible if I'm to make that early start tomorrow – so essential if I'm to get all the way up the narrow ridge to the summit of Mount Hess and back to the col within a single day. One thing's for certain, I daren't go back out onto the ridge again today, not in broad daylight. The bear might see me and get ideas.

I snuggle down deeper inside my sleeping bag. Surrounded by many layers of soft warm fluffy feathers, I'm beginning to get warm at last. I've only got enough food with me to last for the next two whole days, one for the trip to the summit and back, the other for the return journey back down to the Ice Palace. There's a single day's supply of food cached inside the Ice Palace to last me until I can reach my last remaining food supplies at Ravine Camp 3. I'm in a precarious position here regarding supplies, especially if the weather takes a turn for the worse. But I have chosen the rules on this expedition. I'll have no one else to blame if something does go wrong.

I'm only going to take the most basic equipment with me to the summit tomorrow. I must travel as light as possible if I'm to get there and back in a day. My desire to stand on the summit of Mount Hess is so great now that I doubt if anything could stop me. My only hope is for the sun to shine down upon me once I'm on the summit. If this happens I'll be able to go home happy. A climber's world is one of constant cold, which can be enjoyable for itself, but the sun is wonderful also. Dear

THE CLIMB

God! please give me a single moment on the summit of
Mount Hess, with the sun on my face . . .

My gas stove refuses to light. I can't for the life of me see
why. There's going to be no hot meal to send me
happily on my way today. I'll settle for a packet of
chocolate biscuits instead. I'm not going to let anything
bother me because this is the day of the climb. I only
just manage to squeeze through the narrow entrance
hole leading out of my shelter wearing all my bulky
clothing. The sun has just risen above the horizon.
Patchy clouds are racing across the sky. But for now the
weather is good.

I begin to climb directly up the ridge. I continue to
climb precisely on the crest itself for some time. Then I
decide to zigzag, as it becomes wider, to ease the strain
on my legs. It's not long before the ridge narrows down
once more. Then the angle steepens considerably to
slow me down still further. This must be the opportunity I've been waiting for to check that my crampons
are still securely tied onto my boots. But all is well on
this wonderful sunny morning high on the South-West
Ridge of Mount Hess. I continue to climb for hour after
hour, sometimes zigzagging, sometimes taking the slope
more direct. The snow is a perfect consistency this
morning. It's a pleasure to feel my crampons biting hard
into the long curving sweep of the ridge. It's not long
before my first real obstacle confronts me.

A high rock step bars my way.

This step looks for all the world like the wall of some

famous cathedral which has been dumped on a mountain ridge. There's just a single vicious-looking crack, that widens out into a chimney further up, splitting this enormous monolith from top to bottom. Do I really have the nerve to challenge this crack? The alternative is to go around onto extremely steep ice on either side. The degree of difficulty looks about the same. But I find myself being irresistibly drawn towards this savage fissure in the rock. I secure one end of my climbing rope to a long steel piton driven deep into the beginning of the crack, with the other end tied directly into my waist belt. I'm ready to begin climbing now. But first I've got to get a feel for the rock.

I press my hands flat against the hard unyielding surface. (It is obviously trying to intimidate me.) But I'm not going to be frightened by anything today. I start out by jamming the fingers on both my hands into the ever widening crack, with my climbing boots scraping up the featureless rock below me, looking for a foothold, any kind of a hold to support my weight. But there are none to be found anywhere along the edges of this smooth crack. I continue to jam all four fingers on both my hands into the crack, each set of fingers placed directly above the other, with my thumbs into the palms of my hands now for added leverage. It's not long before the crack widens out still further. I'm soon able to get my clenched fists to fit inside the crack. Then the toes of my climbing boots begin to fit neatly inside the split in the rock below me and the strain eases on my arms. I continue to climb higher inside the crack; all the time moving upwards; all the time searching for the top of the high rock step. It's a wonderful feeling to be leaving the ground behind. I watch the lower half of the ridge disappear below me. I'm entering the unknown here. I'm going where no one has ever been before. (At least I think that no one has ever climbed this ridge before.) It's not long before my hands begin to tire. Then just in time the crack opens out to form a wide chimney. I'm able to squeeze the whole of my body up inside it for a well earned rest.

I must secure myself to the rock before I do anything else. I drop a thin tape sling over the top of a convenient spike with a large screw-gate karabiner already attached. Then I clip my main climbing rope into the karabiner. I'm able to relax now, leaning out confidently from the rock on my temporary belay, with my climbing rope pinched double around the bar of the karabiner to help keep me in place. I feel happy now that my belay will turn into the perfect runner once I start climbing again and that, if I fall out of the chimney, it will stop me from hitting the ground. I lean out even further from the safety of the chimney, meaning to study the route ahead. However, my eyes are drawn down towards the glacier. Clouds are boiling up over it but in the gaps there is a set of parallel lines, cut deep into the snow, and standing out in sharp contrast to the more gentle curves of the terrain. I think that in all probability an aircraft must have landed, fitted with a set of wide skis.

If such a landing has taken place on the glacier, there

are bound to be other climbers around, and they should have some spare food with them. I'd welcome even a small amount to supplement my meagre supplies. I've only got a single packet of sweets (soft-centred, sugar-coated, fruit pastilles), a small orange and a bar of chocolate left in my rucksack to eat today. This by any stretch of the imagination cannot be considered to be adequate for a full grown man. I think it would be a good idea if I ate my bar of chocolate now. It is bound to get squashed in my pocket in the struggle to climb out of the chimney.

I've decided upon a new set of rules designed to make my food supplies last longer. I'm only allowed to place one square of chocolate in my mouth at a time. But at the first piece my resolution evaporates with the chocolate and I munch my way through the whole bar. The distinct metallic taste of silver paper, as I lick up the crumbs, lingers on in my mouth as I prepare to climb up the second half of the chimney, heading for the top of the rock step.

Chimneying involves placing my hands flat on the wall behind me, while jamming my knees against the wall in front of me, pushing down with both hands and slowly raising myself, hands and knees in turn, inside the cleft in the rock. It's a painful and slow procedure. However I persevere with my chosen technique until the top of the chimney comes into sight. I carefully pull myself up over the well defined edge and stand up on the ridge. There's only my rope to be released from the piton at the bottom of the pitch and I soon abseil back down for that. It's a pleasure to jumar back up the chimney free from the nightmare of falling off. One of the most serious obstacles on the ridge is behind me. The way ahead is clear. The ridge pulls me onwards. I'm still searching for the summit.

It's not long before I'm forced to stop climbing in order to get my breath back. My lack of acclimatization, because of the sheer speed of my ascent, is beginning to tell on me at last. I take twenty quick lungfuls of crystal clear Alaskan air which gives me the energy needed to start moving off again. But after thirty more steps I'm forced to gasp for breath once more. I kneel down in the snow, with my forehead resting on my ice-axe, driven into the snow in front of me. I feel so exhausted I could almost die. How could I possibly feel any worse than I do? I find my mind drifting away from the task of climbing the mountain. Then my gaze itself begins to falter, wandering down from the point of the ridge, where it should be, until it falls almost out of control, tumbling down through holes in the clouds, past walls of ice, all the way down to the glacier, thousands of metres below me. A silent tremor runs down through my body. There's the clear clang of warning bells ringing loudly in my ears. Take care, David! There can be no mistakes at this height. Just keep on concentrating hard and all will be fine!

I begin to concentrate so hard on climbing up the ridge now that I almost don't notice the high secondary summit of Mount Hess approaching me. It's hard to believe that I've made it as far as this. I begin to zigzag my way carefully up the remaining short section of the ridge towards the secondary summit which has two high points very close together, each surrounded by many tall columns of ice. If you ignore these this secondary summit of Mount Hess is an almost minia-ture version of the beautiful curving summit of the Fletschorn above Saas Grund in Switzerland, although this unusual shape can only be a temporary arrange-ment, formed by wind and storm.

Today must be my lucky day. If I can reach the summit of Mount Hess it will be a fantastic one. If I can get back to my snow cave on the col before the storm strikes, it will be a bloody miracle. Jet black clouds are already racing in towards me from over the Gulf of Alaska. They have completely covered the Talkeetna and Wrangle mountains. The Hayes group are bound to be next. Perhaps it's time I hurried along. The ridge now descends steeply towards another small col, then there's the final short section to climb up to the summit. It's hard to resist a long last lingering look back up at the beautiful secondary summit, because the next time we meet it is bound to be covered by clouds in the approaching storm.

I begin to hurry down towards the col. It's a lot easier going downhill. Today is turning into one of those all too rare balmy days, when I can't seem to put a foot wrong. Feeling like death is forgotten. I must be in perfect form now, or is it simply that I'm going down-hill? Either way, there's a permanent smile on my face.

I stop just once to shout out my arrival to any other

climbers that might be around. Not that I expect to meet anyone up here, with the same great billowing mass of storm clouds racing in towards me, as they have been doing ever since I got up this morning, and the occasional bright spell of sunlight shining down through what little gaps there are. But if I am to meet anyone today, it will be now. The col is roughly the junction with what I take to be the normal route up Mount Hess. It looks the easier approach from the glacier. Anyway, there's no reply to my loud shouts. Still, I don't really mind if I'm going to be all alone, because this is my special day. This wonderful silence can only mean that I have the mountains all to myself. I set out running once more, almost flat out this time, down the final steep section of the ridge, towards the col.

I only just manage to stop in time before the snow turns to ice and I end up flat on my backside. There're just a few marks in the snow, (the grooves made by sharp crampon points, I think) to show me that perhaps some climbers do occasionally pass this way.

My approach to the summit is surrounded in silence. It seems to take me an eternity of slow-motion climbing to reach the highest point on the ridge. I'm finally left standing high on the summit of Mount Hess. I can go no further. The ground drops away steeply on all sides. After all the planning and dreaming and preparing myself for this challenge, I have finally made it. I'm all alone up here on the summit, and that's the way I've always imagined it would be. (There are no climbers to be seen on the various approaches to the summits of Mount Deborah or Mount Hayes either.)

There's no cross to mark out the highest point, as on so many other summits throughout the world, yet this is only fitting. The mountains of Alaska are far too beautiful to be spoilt by man-made objects. In fact, anything placed upon the summit of Mount Hess, no matter how well intentioned, I'm sure would break the spell.

I sit on top of my rucksack and remove my climbing helmet. My face has been burnt brown; my hands have been cut by the ice; but I have made it to the summit of Mount Hess in Alaska and, as if on cue, the sun comes out to turn this wonderful day of mine into a perfect one.

I would never leave anything unnecessary on the summit of any mountain. However, I am allowed to leave the customary message up here, buried deep in the snow inside an empty film container. I wonder if anyone will ever find it. Perhaps a new generation of super climber will stumble across my message, after climbing Mount Hess in half the time that it took me, before he hurries off along the ridge to climb Mount Deborah in time for tea.

It will soon be time for my evening meal, although what the hell I've got left to eat, I don't really know. All I can do is return the way I came, down to the second col, the junction with the normal route up Mount Hess. Then over the high secondary summit to the first col and my food supplies cached there. I take one last lingering look at the magnificent scenery all around me.

To the west, and out of sight, obscured behind the huge summit pyramid of Mount Deborah, there's the Liberty Bell gold mine. Other place names tell their own story of the area: Little Grizzly Creek, Big Grizzly Creek, Caribou Crossing and Grubstake Creek. While over to the north there's the Winter Sled Road, running along the foot of the mountains, giving access by husky dog teams in winter to Blair Lake Air Force Range. While further north, across the banks of the Tanana River lies Fairbanks, founded on gold, and steeped in history. Many place names in the area bear witness to the glittering past of Fairbanks – Goldstream Creek, Nugget Creek – and what I consider to be the most beautiful name of all, Happy Creek. While over to the east there's the vast empty Yukon Territory, stretching out, seemingly, forever. Closer to home, Mount Hayes, the highest mountain in this range, dominates my world. Huge glaciers can be seen radiating out in all directions from the enormous central mass of the mountain to give it a formidable appearance. Beyond the summit of Mount Hayes, and out of sight alongside the Richardson Highway, there are the famous caribou and bison salt licks. Here countless generations of North American reindeer have come to lick their way through hundreds of metric tonnes of salt-laden rocks. To the south, but who the hell wants to look in that direction, there's nothing but a load of jet black storm clouds over there.

I'm ready to leave the summit now. But my boots seem rooted to the ground. It's as if the mountain, having got me up here in the first place, doesn't want to let me go. I certainly haven't climbed Mount Hess to prove anything to anyone. It doesn't matter to me that I may have been the first person to have climbed this particular route, nor who will climb it in the future. Even the degree of difficulty of the South-West Ridge of Mount Hess has no significance to me. I simply climbed it for the oldest of reasons, because it was there, the culmination of a wonderful dream that started out on the summit of Mount Blanc with a wish to escape the crowds and ended here, in Alaska, in victory.

Chapter 8

The Descent

Another race now begins to beat the worsening weather. However, this is one that I lose before it has even begun. The clouds are already surging around me to reduce visibility down to a few short metres. I have that one last lingering look back up at the summit before plunging down the ridge, heading towards the col.

A great mass of wind-blown snow has started to push hard from my left, threatening to hurl me bodily from the ridge. However my speed and determination are far too strong today, nothing must spoil my success, not the wind, not the hail, not even the little piece of ice that has somehow found its way deep into my clothing, nor my aching legs.

I'm tempted to descend the north-facing slope of the mountain at this point. I should be able to reach the glacier more quickly that way, sheltered from the wind. But most of my clothing, my food supplies, and a great deal of my equipment are still inside my shelter on the col. I'm going to need all the food, clothing and equipment I can muster to get me safely back to the Ice Palace. So I'm forced to return the way I came, down the ridge, to the second col, over the secondary summit, then down to the col at the top of the steep ice slope containing my shelter.

The wind continues to tear at my clothing, but I soon leave the flat expanse of the windy col behind me and set off up the ridge as fast as I can. The trail that I made this morning is still clearly visible in the snow. It shows me the safest places to put my feet, but what an effort of will-power it takes to lift my boots up into each step. The last week of strenuous effort is beginning to tell on me at last.

I seem to spend an eternity slipping and sliding in the soft wet snow, then recovering, but always moving forward until my trail ahead vanishes under a weight of falling snow. The storm is well and truly upon me. Where can I safely place my feet now? There's just a great seething mass of snowflakes swirling all around me. I nearly step off the ridge at one point; but I manage to stay in balance with my crampons scraping and scrambling to get a good purchase on the slippery ice. I must cut some steps now. This is the only way that I can safely proceed along the ridge. My staircase gradually begins to take shape. Then, just as my arm begins to tire, the secondary summit of Mount Hess appears in front of me out of the storm clouds. I've reached the top of twin summits at last. But I've still got to find the ridge that will lead me safely down from the summit pyramid onto the col containing my shelter.

The trouble is that I can hardly see my hand in front

of my face now, let alone the ridge. I clearly remember marking the start of my descent route with my ice-hammer stuck in the snow. Where on earth is it now? I continue to walk slowly and carefully around the edge of the summit pyramid, but the ground appears to be falling away steeply on all sides of me. There's no clearly defined ridge to be seen at all. Every feature on the summit pyramid now looks like everything else. I must keep calm here at all costs. I continue to walk around both high points in a huge figure of eight this time, peering intently into the white-out. I've heard others talk about white-outs but never before actually experienced one for myself. It's just like walking around on the inside of an egg.

I'm going to have to stop soon to clean the lenses of my snow-goggles. I step behind the nearest column of ice. But this enormous rectangular block, large though it is, offers me no protection at all. The wind continues to scream across the summit pyramid, driving the snow before it. I'm slowly being turned into a snowman. I reach deep into my trouser pockets for my white cotton handkerchief. But the moment it comes into contact with the ice cold air it freezes solid. I can't get it back into my trouser pocket and have no option but to surrender it to the wind, heading in the direction of the North Pole. But now I've removed the snow from the front of my snow-goggles with the sleeve of my red down jacket, I can see my ice-hammer, sticking up out of the snow and marking the correct route down towards the col.

THE DESCENT

I begin to run down the ridge, heading towards my shelter at the top of the steep ice slope. The high rock step halfway down the ridge is the only remaining obstacle between me and my food supplies on the col. But now there's nothing standing between me and the winds gusting in from the Gulf of Alaska. (I was sheltered from these on the approach to the secondary summit by the huge summit pryamid itself.) The front of my body now takes the full force of these icy cold winds as they try to blow me from the ridge. The cold up here is terrible, as only a ridge several kilometres high in Alaska can be, but my determination to survive is still very strong, and it's this that keeps me moving stubbornly downhill.

It's not long before the top of the high rock step comes into view. Surely this can't be the same one that I climbed only a few hours ago? It seems to go on down through the clouds forever. But of course this is the same one, only I'm more tired, thirsty and hungry now. Any one of these factors has been known to upset one's judgement.

I abseil down the wall of the chimney (completely plastered in snow now), with my rope running hot through my fingers. Powder snow begins to fly everywhere each time my crampons spike through the ice onto the rock. I even manage to smile as my boots strike the ridge beneath me. I immediately let go of my rope, allowing it to spring back up through my hot descendeur. I can't risk burning it.

I try to draw out the last remaining traces of friction

heat from my warm descendeur into my hands. The tips of my fingers feel very cold now. I'm sure that I'm slowly getting frostbite. I'd better find my shelter on the col soon.

I set off down the lower half of the ridge at a run, right into the full force of the wind which seems to be trying to push me back up on top of the twin summits. I'm lifted almost bodily up into the air on top of an exceptionally powerful gust and instinctively spread my arms, trying to keep myself in balance. My climbing boots, heavy though they are, feel like feather weights. Where has gravity gone to? Has it been suspended altogether? If only my arms were wings and I could soar above the storm clouds, as I did in sunny, never to be forgotten, glider-flying days, waiting my turn to fly. "Who, me?" "Yes, you!" repeats the patient flying instructor. "This time try landing back on the runway!" Those were happy days, spent searching for lift of any kind, full of laughter and light, sizzling hot bacon sandwiches and warm cups of coffee afterwards. I'm searching for something very different now. It's a desperate search, on a cold and dark windswept col, in a blinding snowstorm, looking for the entrance to my snow cave, now buried beneath hundreds of metric tonnes of drifting snow.

How is it possible to convey the utter hopelessness of searching for something white in a totally white world. There's the awful realization that if I were to find myself standing right next to my shelter, I still might not see it. I've already lost the feeling in most of my fingers. My situation looks utterly hopeless. If I'm never going to be able to find the entrance to my snow cave in this blinding snowstorm, I've got to leave the col as quickly as possible. I've simply got to descend the complete ice slope, then the glacier, all the way to the Ice Palace. The trouble is I know full well that I'll never make it back to the Ice Palace alive, not after climbing all the way up to the summit of Mount Hess, and then back to the col in a single day. It simply can't be done.

I'd better double-check inside my rucksack now to see what food I do have left. I can't afford to take a wrong decision here. I must not allow myself to be panicked into taking a course of action that I'm going to regret later on. I reach inside my sack and pull out a single packet of soft-centred, sugar-coated, fruit pastilles which is all the food that I've got left to eat. I can't believe there's only a single packet of sweets standing between me and starvation. Is there anything to be gained by saving them for later on? There are just thirteen sugar-coated, multi-coloured treats in a silver paper cylinder. What a performance I have trying to remove the outer wrapping, wearing my thick woollen gloves. I fumble, I curse the tight-fitting silver paper. I daren't take my gloves off, I have to use my teeth. Soon all thirteen pastilles are lying naked and exposed to the full fury of the storm in the palm of my left hand. A whole series of separate explosions occurs as I place each one in turn into my mouth. Thank God there are no white ones in this particular packet. If I were to drop one I'd never find it again. I pop another mouthwatering black currant-flavoured sweet into my mouth. Then a fruity raspberry red. A soft-centred lime tastes just as nice as the others. But an apple-flavoured pastille seems to taste best of all. Soon all thirteen have disappeared. I've gone and eaten the bloody lot. I've got nothing left to eat at all now, and a ball of sweet wrappers in my hand. Where on earth is my next meal going to come from?

There's plenty of time for the snow to pile up against my back as I sit with my back to the wind on top of my rucksack, in what I assume is the middle of the col. But I can't possibly give up searching for the entrance to my shelter. If I give up I'm simply going to die out here. I peer into the lightly falling snowflakes once more. Surely, I tell myself, there must be something different about my shelter, being in part a man-made structure, to distinguish it from the normal features on the col? Now that the storm has eased off a little, I quarter the ground again and, yes, there's a single straight line. There's something sticking up from beneath a bank of snow in the far corner of the col. It has got to be the end of the ski stick I left poking up through the roof of my shelter to keep the ventilation hole open. What a marvellous stroke of luck. This can only be one of those twists of fate that this time is in my favour. If I hadn't left my ski stick sticking up through the roof of my shelter when I did, I'm sure I would never have found the entrance to my snow cave.

The wind is making a terrible noise. It completely disappears the moment I start to seal up the entrance to my shelter. An even greater silence descends over me as the final snow brick fits neatly into place.

The temperature inside my shelter must be somewhere in the region of a few degrees below zero. (It is definitely cold enough to put a thin layer of ice on top of the water inside my water-bottle.) But whatever the temperature is here it must be far colder outside on the col. It's only in these exceptionally cold and windy conditions that the real benefits of living inside a snow cave, as opposed to a tent, start to become apparent. There's plenty of warm calm space available here inside my snow cave in which to sleep and organize myself.

I must get my gas stove working again as a first priority. The last time I tried to use the gas it simply refused to ignite, frozen into silence by the cold, no doubt. I'll solve this problem by taking it into my sleeping bag with me. The ability to melt snow into water is essential, especially at altitude. I'll use some of this water to reconstitute my food and the rest to make hot drinks with. I've still got several small packets of soup left, just waiting to be eaten. But the gas cylinder is taking for ever to thaw out. I light a few candles to warm my fingers up while I'm waiting, cupping my hands around the flames. Tears begin to flow down my cheeks as my circulation gradually returns to normal. At least I've got some feeling back inside my fingers now.

I don't see why I shouldn't use some of my candles to cook with. I could be waiting for ages for the gas cylinder to thaw inside my sleeping bag. Leaning out from the security of my sleeping bag, I begin to scrape the snow from the walls of my shelter with the sharp edges of my cooking pan, then I light more candles and hold the pan steady over them with both hands. I bring my face closer in towards the warm candle flames once more. I could hold it in this super warm position forever. I close my eyes against the heat as the snow inside my cooking pan slowly begins to melt. Steam rises to fill every corner of my shelter. I'm starting to get warm at last. I open my eyes to peer inside my cooking pan. The water is starting to boil now. I search around for my sachet of coffee in one of the wall alcoves of my shelter. I must be careful not to singe my eyebrows here. I move further back from the candle flames.

But what on earth is happening to my cooking pan? A thick black smoke has started to appear around its sides. It is slowly turning black! Good God! My cooking pan is covered all over in soot now. The candles have created one hell of a sooty mess. I quickly remove the pan from the flames. I lay it down on the icy floor of my shelter, where the bottom immediately begins to melt down into the snow. But it's too late to stop the walls of my shelter from turning black. I must get rid of the smoke before I choke to death. I enlarge the ventilation hole in the roof. Mustn't make it too large or I'll freeze. The smoke soon clears, but I haven't moved fast enough to stop the outside of my cooking pan from turning completely black.

My one consolation is that the water hasn't been affected, so I make my coffee and sip gingerly straight from the pan. The sudden exertion forced upon me by the crisis with my cooking pan has made me feel very tired indeed. I should be making a real effort to cook something to eat. However, a drink of coffee will do for now, my evening meal can wait till later.

My body aches all over from the hard physical effort of the last few days. I've hardly dared to rest on any stage of this expedition. The fact that I can only carry a limited amount of food with me lies at the heart of most of my problems. I've simply got to keep all my activities within the limits set by my food supplies. I must ruthlessly adhere to my schedule now if I'm to survive.

It's at moments like this one might be tempted to wonder what motivated me to climb Mount Hess in the first place. But I know the answer. I could have turned around and gone back to the Denali Highway at any time on the approach to the mountain. It would be difficult to imagine a more worthless venture, if one were to quantify my expedition purely in material terms. The simple fact is that I find climbing enjoyable for itself and something that I must do. Soon I'll be back home in Kingston-upon-Hull, working as a highways foreman with the local council, trying to earn enough money to finance my next expedition. Back home I'll be surrounded by the usual flat and boring landscape, where someone seeing me gazing into the night sky may doubt my sanity. But I'll know what I'll be doing. I'll be dreaming, planning and laughing away to myself, only my laughter will be that of a climber who really was there.

THE DESCENT

My candles begin to flicker. It won't be long now before they go out completely. I'm suddenly left all alone in a world of darkness. My consolation is that the gas cylinder on my stove has warmed up at last. I must make an effort to cook something. All I have to do is reach out from my sleeping bag for a box of matches. But I know full well that no part of me is going to leave the warmth of my sleeping bag until morning. I'm far too tired even to care that I'm ravenously hungry. I'm definitely not moving.

I dreamt that I was eating a large rump steak last night. Instead I mix all the different flavoured soups together on my now well behaved gas stove. I take a cautious sip. Surely there's the hint of long forgotten potato and leek in there somewhere, along with many other wonderful flavours. I continue to stir the thickening mixture with the tip of my ice-axe. It'll all add to the flavour. Another long hot tongue-burning sip, straight out of the pan. There was some oxtail in that one. It ends up tasting more like plain vegetable soup than anything else, one of my favourites. This is one meal that I'll remember for a long time to come. I pack my gas stove inside my rucksack.

I've only got one small orange left to eat now. I'll have it for dessert. I peel it with all the care of a surgeon performing a delicate operation, but trying to make the process last as long as possible. Once I've eaten my orange, that's it. The trouble is that I still feel hungry and my nearest food supplies are down at the Ice Palace.

Then there's my last remaining food cache back in the ravine. There's no time to waste.

I fasten my crampons onto my boots and blow out the last remaining candle. The pungent smell of smoke from the smouldering wick lingers in my nostrils as I squeeze through the narrow entrance tunnel leading out of my shelter. It's a relief to see that the weather conditions have improved at last.

My tunnel through the heart of the cornice is still there, ready to lead me out onto the steep ice slope. Descending the tunnel is very much like going down a slide in a children's playground, feet first, the only difference being that I have to remember to stop at the bottom.

I revel in the exposure facing me on the steep ice slope. "Make it steeper," I whisper silently to myself, after kicking in the front-points on my crampons. But the angle soon eases off, obliging me to turn around and face out from the slope. I can see where I'm going at last, were it not for a mass of cloud blotting out the entire glacier basin below me.

I begin to make longer and longer glissades over the surface of the snow, just as it begins to soften up a little. I'm admiring myself swooping down the slope, using my boots like skis again. I make another highly pleasurable long looping turn over the surface of the snow. A crevasse looms up out of the mist. I jump it, almost without pausing. What a marvellous feeling of strength and power. Nothing can stop me now. I'm going to ski all the way down to the glacier on the soles of my boots.

Fortunately, commonsense overtakes euphoria and I turn my boots well over to one side in the wet snow on the very edge of a huge crevasse. This is one I would never have successfully jumped across.

As I walk along the lip, looking for a way across, I begin to pass hundreds of small black specks in the snow. When I kneel down I discover they're insects lying motionless in amongst the ice crystals, wings frozen in flight, having apparently had no choice in their final destination. But it's snowbridges that I want to be finding now, not insects.

I find myself being forced further over to one side of the steep ice slope, until suddenly the northernmost retaining wall looms up out of the mist. There's a clearly defined ridge here, mostly rocks and clear of snow. It offers me a route down onto the glacier, all the way down if I really wanted to follow the ridge in its entirety. I sit down on top of my rucksack to decide what to do for the best. I'd prefer to stay with the ice slope, but I daren't jump across the crevasse. So I decide to follow the ridge all the way down to the glacier.

My fingers fall into the first tall crack that comes to hand and I move quickly down the smooth face of the rock; stepping down all the time, getting closer to the glacier all the time.

There's a void beneath my feet to contend with now. This crevasse, separating the ice slope from the flank of the ridge, is not unusually wide or deep, but the thought of falling into it makes me shudder. This fear of falling has been with me for as long as I can remember. The first few days of any climbing holiday are usually the worst, then I soon get used to the void. I'm not helped in any way by living and working in an area that is, by mountaineering standards, flat. I never get to see a real drop from one day to the next.

It was in my own home city of Kingston-upon-Hull, in my first job after leaving school as an apprentice sheet metal worker (at J. G. Pickerings Ltd) that I realized for the first time just how afraid of heights I really was. During the dinner-hour my workmates would race one another up onto the flat roof of an empty warehouse alongside where we worked, via a large metal-runged fire-escape to play a game of football up there. I would deliberately hang back, placing myself last in the line. I would never get more than about twenty steps up the fire-escape before the most awful dread would come over me. I'd literally shake from head to foot before retreating the short distance that I had managed to climb back down to the ground. No one will ever know just how hard I tried to climb that long line of fire-escape steps to the top of the building.

Something just had to be done about it. Those steps up the side of the building were to become my Everest, my Eiger Nordwand, although at the time I'd never heard of the great north face on this last mountain. To climb those hundred or so steps to the top of the building was a challenge that was to take over my every waking moment. Over the weeks and months that followed, more and more of those shiny metal steps were to fall beneath my feet. I grew bolder each time I attempted to climb up the fire-escape until, suddenly, there were no more steps left to climb. Finally I stepped up onto the roof. I had beaten my fear of heights at last, or so I thought. I ran across to join the others in their game of football. But something was definitely wrong. This game, that I'd wanted to join for so long, seemed positively boring to me now. Instead I was being drawn into the world of climbing. The wall of any building in Kingston-upon-Hull seemed to pull me like a piece of metal to a magnet. No wall was safe from my hands. I was becoming well and truly hooked. Climbing just had to become a larger part of my life. The pavement was for others. They could remain eyes fixed upon the ground. I would reach out for the stars. It was as if I had been finally released from the earth forever.

A small movement on the ridge above me forces me to look up. I stop climbing and remain watching the crest of the ridge for some time. After a while, I think I must have been mistaken and continue to traverse down the side of the ridge, moving left all the time, losing height all the time in my descent towards the glacier.

I place my hands around a generous pair of jug holds, then another. I begin to feel safe now. With so many large handholds I can't possibly fall off. Suddenly there is a noise from above. I freeze in place. The wall of rock in front of me begins to shake. I grip my large handholds even tighter now, as the first huge boulder comes bouncing into view above me. I place my rucksack on top of my head and shout out an almost instinctive,

"Below!" to warn any other climbers that might be around. But there are no other people around to hear my shout. I watch helplessly as the leading boulder impacts the side of the ridge just a short distance above me. I close my eyes. I can't bear to look. The huge boulder instantly explodes into a thousand tiny scream-ing fragments of rock. Large pieces ricochet off the flank of the ridge all around me, then hurtle on to gouge out craters in the ice slope below. Smaller slabs follow on behind this huge leading boulder, with some coming perilously close to my climbing helmet. An awesome silence hangs over the ridge as the avalanche stops. I peep cautiously around the sides of my ruck-sack, but nothing happens. Nothing is moving around me either. A huge cloud of rock dust hangs in the air below my feet.

I'm in no hurry to move away from my super safe pair of jugs, fearful that any movement I make will upset some delicate balance in nature and start off another avalanche. At least the avalanche debris has now filled in the gap between the two enormous walls of the crevasse and, unstable though it is, offers me a way across the gap back on to the ice slope once more. But do I have the courage to walk across it? One thing's for certain here, I've lost my nerve for climbing down the side of the ridge. I'll feel a lot safer back on the ice slope. One huge rectangular block of granite in particular, jammed in between the walls of the crevasse, tempts me over.

I abseil down on top of it and jump up and down to

test it, protected by my rope from above. Not a single pebble moves out of its place as I tiptoe my way slowly and carefully across the bridge.

I'd better climb up the wall of ice on the far side quickly before any more debris comes down. I'm sure I can hear a noise above. A small fragment of rock comes bouncing down the side of the ridge, as if to confirm my worst fears. It makes a hole as neat as any bullet in the ice alongside me. I don't need any prompting now. I literally hurl myself up at the wall of ice forming the side of the steep ice slope, with both axes in use as the top of the crevasse looms up, and start to run. This is the proverbial calm before the storm. I've often found it to be the case that nature tends to repeat itself, and never more so than with avalanches. They seem to be in the same places, time after time, with only the precise moment of the avalanche itself in doubt.

As if to prove my point another rock comes bouncing down the side of the ridge. It clatters down into the crevasse behind me. However this second rock bounces out. I only just manage to jump out of its path. It misses my right leg by a whisker. I run even faster now, as fast as the sloping surface of steep ice will allow, and am eventually out of range as the second avalanche rains down, released by the heat of the sun, after being pushed out by the ever expanding ice.

The glacier can't be that far below me now. But it's so hard to see anything through the mist and to make matters worse it begins to snow. My boots cut a neat trail in the snow behind me. However, it's not long before the snow fills it in and there's nothing to be seen of my trail any more. Suspicious hollows appear in front of me to speed me on my way. Then the mist suddenly parts to reveal a large expanse of the Main West Fork Glacier a short distance below. There's just the bergschrund to cross now. This huge crevasse at the bottom of the steep ice slope is the only obstacle between me and my food supplies some fourteen kilometres down the glacier back at the Ice Palace.

Chapter 9

Walking into a Trap

I begin to make a new trail in the snow. There may be a bear coming up my old one! It's a daunting prospect, compacting the snow at every step, but I don't really mind, it's better than meeting my old enemy. My one consolation is that it's all downhill from now on.

The snow is melting now as summer approaches, and I begin to sink deeper with each stride. The snow sticks like glue to the metal frames beneath my crampons. It's time to take them off and put my snowshoes back on. What a relief. I start to float over the shiny surface into the mist. Mount Hess and the high mountains have disappeared behind me. It's almost as if I've been the intruder here and, now that I've left the mountains behind, their silence can return.

My complete world is now contained within a small circle of brilliant white sunlight, filtering down to me. To ease my aching shoulders I take the rope from the top of my rucksack and trail it behind me. It's the perfect climbing companion, letting me do all the talking, never disagreeing with any decision that I make. We halt together, we move off together.

The clouds part and it's a great relief to see where I'm going at last. At some point I've got to cross over to the other side of the glacier. I wish I knew when to do this. The trouble is that the Main West Fork Glacier is such a big one. It would take only the smallest error in my route-finding for me to get completely lost. I could even find myself going around in circles. I'm still a little uncertain about the best way forward.

I come to an enormous lake, the largest expanse of water that I've seen on any glacier. You could stage a sailing regatta on it. I can't remember seeing this lake marked on one of my maps. Or have I? I'm sure I haven't passed one as big as this on the way up here. I could of course be mistaken on both accounts and after losing both my maps and compass in the avalanche that swept across the top of the Ice Palace, I've no way of checking now.

But wherever I am, it is a breathtaking sight as the sun's rays hit each individual iceberg in turn, reflecting prisms of harvest gold, morning primrose, poppy red, purple and deep-space Alaskan blue. The vision holds me spellbound by its sheer beauty. But where is this place in the great scheme of things? Seeing such an enormous expanse of water has thrown my normally ordered mind into a complete and utter confusion.

If only I could somehow create my own compass in the snow, then at least I would be able to start out in the right direction. But in order to do that I need to find out what the time is. I can still see the sun quite clearly through a small gap in the clouds directly in front of me. It looks to be a few hours past its highest midday point in the sky, so the time must be somewhere in the region of 2 p.m. in the afternoon. I begin to draw a circular clock face in the snow using the spike of my ice-axe to great effect. I mark out a small hour hand on the clock face, pointing straight at the direction of the sun and the number 2. Then I draw a minute hand pointing at the number 12. The time, 2 p.m., is now clearly written in the snow. I step back to admire my handiwork. The diameter of my clock face is enormous. I wonder what the pilot of an aircraft passing directly overhead would make of it, especially if he were to fly over the clock face at 2 p.m. precisely. My clock would appear to be telling him the time! But this is not a clock for telling the time. It's a compass for pointing the way. I need to cross the glacier in a north-westerly direction in order to find my food supplies back at the Ice Palace. I walk carefully around the circumference of my clock face until I reach a point halfway between the numbers 12 and 2, then turn to face in to the centre of the circle. I must be facing north now, having bisected the angle formed by the number 12 and 2, and from this I can determine the north-west and continue my journey with more confidence.

I jump a couple of crevasses, slide down some moraine banks and navigate round ice towers. A cloud of fine rock dust hangs in the air behind me as I descend the third and final moraine bank at a run. Then suddenly a high wall of rock looms up out of the mist. I can't believe it. I've crossed the complete width of the glacier blind. The Ice Palace and my food supplies can't be far from here. I am looking for three tall cairns, the ones I erected close to the glacier entrance leading down inside the Ice Palace. I keep expecting to see them appear in front of me at any moment.

As I stare ahead into the swirling mist, I fantasize about the aroma of sausages, eggs and bacon. I imagine it drifting up the glacier. I could do with some beans on my plate as well. A slice of lamb's liver would fit nicely alongside my beans. These fabulous thoughts sustain me in my search, though in reality there's only a single box of dehydrated food cached at the Ice Palace. But I am allowed to dream.

How I long to smell food of any description now. However I can definitely perceive something unpleasant drifting up the glacier. There's the distinct smell of rotting meat being carried towards me on the breeze, a dank musty odour that seems to cling to everything, is strangely familiar to me, yet inexplicable. At that moment I break to a knee-jarring stop on the edge of an ice cliff. I break out into a cold sweat. I almost stepped over the edge of it. I'll just have to be more careful in future and stop day-dreaming about food. But I have stumbled upon, almost into, my beautiful ice lake, and opposite me now there's the large pear-shaped opening, my lower entrance, via the watercourse tunnel, down inside the Ice Palace. I can see the three cairns on the other side of the lake now. Everything falls into place. I've found the Ice Palace. I've found my food supplies at last.

There are more boulders than I remember scattered around the glacier entrance leading down inside the Ice Palace. Perhaps another avalanche has swept over the top of my shelter while I've been away? I stand up on top of one huge boulder, trying to puzzle it out. There's a scene of utter devastation surrounding me. Debris radiates out in all directions from my entrance tunnel. The rope is still there, still secured to its boulder. But this tunnel opening was definitely blocked two days ago when the floor of the ramp collapsed. It is completely clear of debris now.

I walk over to the edge of the hole leading down into the Ice Palace, weaving a careful route around the debris. I lie down flat on my stomach peering down into the void. I can't see a bloody thing. It's very dark inside the ramp. I must give my eyes time to get used to the darkness. Very slowly and gradually the walls come into focus. The ramp is completely empty of debris now. I can even see the entrance to my sleeping chamber in the half-light at the bottom.

I still can't find any rational explanation for all this upheaval, but I'm more concerned with the floor of the ramp at the moment. I've no wish to fall back through the hole in the floor a second time. I daren't take too many chances here. I'll simply bridge across between the walls of the ramp in order to get back inside my sleeping chamber, avoiding the floor completely.

I lower myself down inside the hole in the glacier

with the sharp points along the outer edges of each of my crampons biting hard into the walls of ice on either side of me, my hands pressed flat against the ice. I continue to step my hands down the sloping walls of the crevasse, until my fingers come up against a set of long thin grooves cut deep into the ice, then lower down another. Surely these long thin grooves can only be claw marks? Only a bear has the power to cut into the ice like that. It must have been waiting for me out on the glacier a few nights ago when I was asleep inside my sleeping chamber. It doesn't take any stretch of my imagination to figure out that it must be the same bear that has been following me. It can only be Scar Face.

It's frightening to think that a bear was creeping about on the glacier, only a short distance above my head, just waiting for me to emerge from my shelter. The bear must have started to tunnel down inside the ramp after I'd left, unaware that I wasn't inside the Ice Palace any more, that I'd left by the other entrance down by the lake. It must have worked itself up into a fury after following my trail up the glacier, burrowing deep into the ramp, hurling aside massive blocks of snow and ice, as if they were mere feather weights. Everything falls into place now, including the smell of rotting meat out on the glacier. Most bears smell to a degree of decaying flesh. There's not the slightest doubt in my mind now that it still has every intention of killing me.

I freeze in my tracks, still bridged tightly between the two walls of the ramp, with a terrible fear pulsing through my body. The full horror of what has been happening suddenly dawns on me. It's obvious to me now that the bear is still following me. It could even be inside the Ice Palace, returning here after failing to climb across the bergschrund, and be waiting for me at the bottom of the ramp, just around the corner, inside my sleeping chamber.

The bear could be almost anywhere!

I can't afford to get caught inside the close confining walls of the ramp. I must get out of here before the bear comes back, then get my rope down the wall of ice surrounding the lake. If it does return, at least I'll have somewhere safe to go. I can simply climb down my rope. I can only hope that the bear's not already inside one of the tunnels down there waiting for me. I've got to enter the Ice Palace sooner or later in order to get at my food supplies.

My heart pounds in my chest after climbing out of the ramp and running across the glacier, where I quickly lower my rope down the ice wall right into the lake, jumping nervously as the end of my rope hits the water. A whole series of small ripples spread out over the surface and I watch each one rock a different iceberg in turn.

My attention is diverted by a new noise, behind some blocks of ice some several hundred metres to my left. I don't think that it's a good idea to wait around up here any longer. I start to climb down my rope, lowering myself slowly down the wall of ice, until my eyes are left peeping out over the surface of the glacier.

There's still no sign of the bear. A stone must have fallen into a crevasse. Small pebbles are falling all the time on any glacier. I think I'll climb further down my rope. There's no point in me watching the glacier, looking for a bear that's no longer around.

But what if the bear is inside the Ice Palace waiting for me to return? I can see that I might have to run for it when I eventually decide to enter the Ice Palace in order to get at my food supplies. I can only hope that it doesn't come to a race up my rope with the bear chasing after me. I feel safe for the moment, hanging halfway up the wall of ice surrounding the lake, with the water lapping gently against the bottom of the wall, just a few short metres below me. But am I really safe from a bear? It has such long forelegs. There are, after all, only a few metres of wall above and below me. But where is the bear now? All I can say for certain is that it has definitely been inside the Ice Palace. I only wish that it would hurry up and show itself. But surely the bear would have attacked me by now if it was still around? My only hope is that it has gone away because sooner or later I'm going to have to leave the safety of my rope and enter the Ice Palace.

I think I'd better act now before I lose my nerve completely, although a strange thing has happened, my craving for food has completely disappeared. It must be fear. However the moment I swing back inside the long watercourse tunnel my hunger returns. I remain perfectly still for some time listening for any sound that might betray the presence of the bear. There's no sound, only the most terrible smell. This pungent odour can only be bear. At least I know for sure now that it has been all the way through the complete set of tunnels making up the Ice Palace. I'm almost thrown into a blind panic by the mere thought that it could be waiting for me somewhere inside my shelter. I switch my headtorch on. The strong white beam parts the darkness in front of me and the presence of the light helps to reassure me that all is well. There's no sign of the bear inside the long watercourse tunnel. After the fear inducing click of my headtorch going on the silence returns to haunt me. Only this time it becomes deeper and deadlier than ever before.

I begin to edge my way slowly and carefully forward along the dish-shaped floor of the long watercourse tunnel. My crampons spike hard into the icy floor of the stinking tunnel. There are plenty more claw marks to be seen. I stop a few metres short of the hole I have to climb through into the next tunnel and listen for a while. There's no noise. I climb up into the short curving tunnel. I stop to listen once more, flattening myself against the wall. I hardly dare breathe as I slowly edge my way forward around the corner of the tunnel, only too fearful of what I might see. But my sleeping chamber is completely empty. I've got to get a grip on myself. I must check inside the ramp now as a first priority. I wade through the debris on the floor, place my hands on either side of the entrance and look up the full length of the tunnel. There's no bear inside the ramp.

But where has my food parcel got to? I turn around. The light from my headtorch illuminates the ground. The floor of my sleeping chamber is covered in small pieces of paper. My food parcel has been torn to shreds. The contents are scattered all over the floor of my shelter. There's a small yellow stain high in one wall. This can only be the remains of my orange. The bear must have pounded it into the wall with its massive front paws. My orange has almost become part of the glacier now. The same is true of every other item in my food parcel. Even the wrapping paper torn from one of my chocolate bars has been stomped into the ground by the bear. It's as if it has tried to destroy every last vestige of me. The claw and fist marks of the creature are everywhere.

Surely the bear must have overlooked something? I can't believe it has destroyed every item of food. I must begin a systematic search. I might still be able to find my tin of pilchards. I've got to believe I can find something to eat or I'll lose all hope of getting out of here alive. I must get some decent food inside me if I'm to survive the journey back to Ravine Camp 3.

Down on my hands and knees, I begin to claw at the boulders frozen into the floor which must have rolled down when the ramp collapsed. Nothing. I suddenly begin to feel very cold indeed. I lean back up against the wall of my shelter in a state of complete and utter despair. Why has my expedition to end like this? I've been plagued with the problem of carrying enough food to eat.

The cold from the wall of ice behind me penetrates my many layers of clothing, to freeze the very life out of me. I couldn't care less what the cold does to me any more.

The pencil thin beam of my headtorch plays upon the claw marks on the opposite wall. Then I notice a small packet jammed into a crack. This can only be a packet of potato flakes. I've got some food to eat at last! The effect of this single packet of potato flakes on my morale is electrifying. I'll have some real mashed potato to eat now. But I daren't prepare food inside my shelter with a bear roaming about on the glacier. They can smell food cooking from a distance of several kilometres. I've got no choice but to cook my potato flakes later on tonight, once I've found somewhere safe and warm to sleep.

The weather outside is still quite reasonable. It's important, therefore, that I travel as far as I possibly can down the glacier, trying to reach the snow slope that will eventually lead me back up onto the ridge overlooking Ravine Camp 3. If I get caught out on the glacier in a real storm with no decent food left to eat, I will have had it.

But what about my survival candles? I've forgotten that I've placed two of them in the walls of my shelter. I can always eat them as a last resort. When I first heard about candles that you could eat at the Scout Shop in Hull I'd laughed at the idea, but I'm not going to do that again. I think I'd better ration them out now. I cut them both in half. One piece for each of the next four days that it will probably take me to get back to the Denali Highway.

The exit from the long watercourse tunnel soon appears in front of me. I pass another set of huge paw prints, with the claw marks clearly visible at the front of each wide depression. The sight of all these claw marks on the floor of the tunnel makes me shudder. And surely that can't be a pile of bear shit in the centre of the narrow channel? How on earth could I have missed it on the way up here? All I can do now is hope and pray that I don't end up as part of a similar pile after becoming the bear's next meal.

I stick my head very cautiously out of the entrance to the tunnel, I'm still looking for any sign that the bear might be watching me. The late afternoon sunlight is brilliant after the darkness inside my shelter and I quickly pull my snow-goggles down over my eyes. Huge blocks of ice, big enough to be called icebergs, continue to float around on the super calm waters of the lake below me under the full glare of the sun. It seems to bring everything that it touches to life, including me. I've spent far too much time underground on this expedition. I'll spend my next one in the sunniest place that I can find.

My rope is still there, hanging straight down, in front of me, with the end trailing in the lake below. The end of my rope seems to have become the centre of attraction for numerous small pieces of paper floating about on the water. I'm sure there was no debris of any kind in the water when I first arrived here. I can only assume that this rubbish is the remains of my food parcel.

Clearly the bear made this mess and I'm going to have to find a way to clear it up. I'd never be able to live with myself if I didn't leave the lake in the same pristine condition that I found it. I'm fortunate in that the bear has ripped several enormous chunks of ice out of the sides of the tunnel in its rage. I'll try throwing these at the rubbish and hope to sink it that way. I pick up the nearest chunk of ice ready to drop it down on top of a green coloured piece of vegetable soup wrapping. As I take aim, it suddenly moves away, while several more pieces come floating towards the rope end on the crest of a huge wave.

It's the bear! I should have heard the splash! It must have been watching me from behind one of the blocks of ice in the centre of the lake. I should have realized. Everything falls into place now. The claw marks on the walls of the tunnel, the great big pile of bear shit, the debris in the water, deposited there by the bear's claws after ripping my food parcel to shreds. The bear must have swum out to one of the ice blocks and simply waited there for me to return.

The powerful body of the bear seems to cut through the water as if it weren't there at all. It is swimming straight towards me. I slip on the floor of the tunnel in my haste to grasp hold of my rope, still hanging straight down in front of me. I scramble to my feet. I glance down at the bear. A huge wave of water is rising up on either side of the bear's two gigantic shoulders, and central to these two waves, spearheading the charge towards me, is a pair of the most evil eyes that I have ever seen. The look on the bear's scarred face fills me with a terrible fear. I know how fast it can move. I'm just going to have to be quicker. My feet slip once more as I grasp my rope and swing out over the lake. My hands begin to slip back down my icy rope. Fortunately one of the knots stops me from slipping any further. The bear lunges up at me. I lift my legs high in the air. I hug my knees close to my chest. But it misses them at its first attempt, falling backwards into the water beneath me with a tremendous splash. I must get higher up my rope before it has time to recover, but I don't think I'm going to make it. The bear's claws hook into the ice just a short distance below me as it powers up out of the water once more. The ice groans. Then a huge chunk rips out of the wall, taking the bear backwards with it. The bear, with the ice still fixed to its long claws, falls backwards into the water with another enormous splash. The water in the lake heaves high up into the air, creeping up the ice below me, over the top of my climbing boots, then up the lower part of my legs. My climbing breeches are soaked now. But I don't care how wet they are because the bear has missed me. The water drains off into my watercourse tunnel and I pull myself up my rope as fast as I possibly can.

The bear wastes no time in coming back at me, swimming through the water with all the power and agility for which giant grizzlies are notorious. I sweat with the effort of trying to keep my hands in place on my icy climbing rope. They begin to slip once more, so do my dripping boots. But I'm well out of reach of the bear's long forelegs and it falls backwards with another mighty splash. I can clearly feel the cold pressure wave of air on top of the next huge surge of water rising up the wall of ice beneath me. I daren't stop to turn around to see how far the water has progressed, or where the bear has landed, every second is going to count here. I quickly pull myself up over the edge of the high ice cliff surrounding the lake, only just managing to escape the second huge surge of water rising up the wall of ice beneath me. I collapse forward onto my hands and knees in the snow. I must get my breath back before I do anything else. But I daren't stop to recover. I can't possibly rest here knowing that the bear is trying to climb out of the lake.

My heart pounds in my chest as I run towards the glacier entrance leading down into the Ice Palace. The bear might already be heading up the tunnels in that direction, for all I know, with ideas of using the ramp to get out. I must trap it down by the lake once and for all. I must cage it within the high walls of ice surrounding the lake forever. I sweat with the effort of rolling another huge block of ice down through the hole in the glacier and onto the sloping floor of the ramp. I hardly dare stop to look behind me now as I continue to push the rocks and blocks of ice down through the hole, gradually filling it up with debris, until I'm satisfied that the ramp is completely blocked with sufficient boulders and blocks of ice to imprison the bear down by the lake forever.

My breathing gradually returns to normal, but I can still hear the bear panting down in the lake. When it subsides there's nothing but the most awful deathly silence surrounding us both. I walk slowly back towards the edge of the high ice cliff and look down. The bear is lying flat on its stomach on top of a block of ice in the exact centre of the lake. The expression on its face now is one of sullen indifference. Still the bear can't reach me now. I'm the one that's standing safely on top of the high wall of ice. The bear's the one that's trapped in the middle of the lake. But what a monstrous creature this is, truly a king of beasts.

I can understand the bear wishing to take vengeance. I can understand any creature wishing to do just that. The bear has seen me now and its gaze doesn't falter. The bear's ears prick up when I begin to speak to it. I try to explain my reasons for what happened to its cub in the clearing. I hear myself desperately trying to put my side of the story, apologizing for murder. The bear's eyes remain locked onto mine. It's a terrible, savage, silent look, one that seems to be demanding the total annihilation of an enemy. I can see that there's going to be no surrender here. It still has every intention of killing me. But the bear can't do anything to me now. It is trapped down there forever.

I only manage to take a few steps forward along my trail when the ground begins to shake beneath my feet. I turn back towards the top of the ice cliff. A huge column of water is falling back into the lake. What on earth has the bear been doing in the few moments that I've been away? I watch it swim back towards its ice block. It must have waited until my back was turned, then swum across to throw itself at the wall before falling back into the water again after failing to climb out of its cage. The bear is never going to be able to climb such a high wall of ice. It is a constant nine metres in height throughout its length and there are no gaps. I back off. Large pieces of ice are crumbling away from where I am standing as the bear climbs back on its huge block of ice, sending it slowly spinning. What kind of awesome power does it take to send an iceberg spinning and a glacier trembling? Just one look at the horrendous expression on the bear's face is enough to send me scurrying back out of sight.

I must forget about the bear now. I must get as far as I possibly can down the glacier while the weather is still reasonable. I've got a powerful wind at my back, and can follow the trail that I made on the way up. In the deepest snow, the clear imprints of my snowshoes can be seen, in more shallow snow conditions, the marks made by my boots, with the vibram pattern on the soles showing up in sharp relief, while a whole series of small holes in the ice show where I was using crampons. But whatever the conditions that existed on the ground, at the time, and the footwear that I used, the trail that I made on the way up is a sure one to follow in the gathering darkness. It's a marvellous feeling to be able to follow a trail in relative safety, with most of the holes having been found the first time around. I weave my way around another set of crevasses, still following my trail in the snow precisely. I clearly remember negotiating this particular system on the way up.

But I don't remember seeing another trail close to mine. There's definitely one, going up the glacier, over on my left. I walk across to satisfy my curiosity. What an enormous one it turns out to be. This great trench in the snow is far too deep to have been made by another human being. The bear must have made this trail, following me up the glacier. But I'll not let it go to waste. The trail, being deeper than mine, should be easier to follow. My boots begin to fit into the bear's own huge paw prints exactly, at every second step. Who will ever believe me when I say that I'm actually beginning to feel like a bear myself as I walk in its prints. If anything, I'm starting to experience something of the bear's own rolling gait. There are three ways that a bear travels over the ground: an even deliberate gait to take it over rough terrain; a quick shuffle, that can be used almost anywhere; and a very fast gallop, that can reach an all out sixty-five kilometres per hour when chasing its prey. One thing's for sure, walking in the bear's footsteps is beginning to have a very strange effect on me.

The sun gradually disappears below the horizon, a light snow has just started to fall finding its way up the sleeves of my red down jacket and inside my gloves, and the wind has changed direction. I try to present as small a target as possible to the snow being blown towards me. Large areas of my trail have already begun to disappear completely, filled to the top with drifting snow. It's time I called it a day. My luck holds out and I stumble into a large cavern inside an even larger tower of ice. The silence inside this monstrous block of ice is deafening after the roar of the wind outside. By my failing headtorch I glimpse numerous slim stalagmite columns of ice growing up out of the floor all around me and there are stalactites growing down from the roof of my shelter, a ready made water supply which I can melt down into water far more quickly than collecting snow from outside. A few taps with my ice-axe is all that's needed to bring more icicles crashing down beside me as I lie inside my sleeping bag, with the ice inside my pan melting gently on top of my gas stove.

Whatever I do I mustn't burn my potato flakes. I reach out from the warmth of my sleeping bag once more to turn the gas jets down as I watch them swell. I'm going to have some decent food to eat at last. I'll add a small pinch of salt. I only wish that I had a knob of butter to add as well. But a slice of fat taken from one of my edible candles does the job fine. This is food fit for any climber. My only wish is that I had some more of it. I've no idea where my next meal is going to come from. My candles only count as emergency rations. The calorific value of three small pieces of white candle wax is far too small to enter into this life and death equation. But I'm reasonably happy now after eating my evening meal of warm potato flakes.

I try to go to sleep, but I can't, it's far too cold inside my shelter. There are far too many freezing cold arrows stabbing up at me from the ice floor beneath me, and from the frigid air all around me. The cold seems to have penetrated my clothing on all sides, now that the effect of my hot meal has worn off. I've simply got to put into practice every lesson that I've ever learnt over years of climbing if I'm to survive the night. I empty my belongings out of my rucksack and pull it up over the lower half of my sleeping bag to warm my legs. Then I pull my cagoule down over my head and shoulders and the top half of my body, still inside my sleeping bag. I have a terrible struggle trying to enclose everything surrounding me. I wriggle my toes to get my circulation going again. The cold is even starting to affect the new batteries I've just put inside my headtorch which are slowly being drained of their power. I should really reach out to switch my headtorch off in order to conserve what's left. But I know full well that if I were to reach out what little warmth there is inside my sleeping bag would simply disappear. I watch the light from my headtorch grow dim. Then suddenly it goes out completely. I'm left all alone in a world of darkness.

The only sensation reaching me now is the annoying sound of water dripping down onto the outer plastic cover of my emergency bivouac sack from an icicle high above me. This repetitive sound is going to drive me to distraction if I don't do something about it soon. But again that would involve getting out of my sleeping bag. It's far more important for me to keep what little warmth there is where it belongs, surrounding me. This dripping sound, annoying though it is, is only a secondary consideration. I'll let nature take its course. As the night wears on any water still left inside my shelter will be frozen into silence.

Chapter 10

Nightmare

All the previously hidden features on the glacier now come into sharp focus in the early morning sunshine as I bound on my way. Most worrying are the numerous avalanche cones, another good reason to drive on relentlessly in anticipation of a decent meal down at Ravine Camp 3. Unfortunately, the clouds and mist have returned once more. The sun has never stayed out for long enough on this expedition. A few hours here and there, this has so far been the pattern of my holiday. But the lack of any real sunshine is not the main reason for my complaints about the weather. These misty cloudy conditions will make it very difficult for me to find the correct ice slope that will take me off the glacier. If I'm not careful I could lose my way here completely and find myself climbing up the wrong ice slope, leading down into the wrong valley. I try to put this terrible thought to the back of my mind as I confront my first serious crevasse, deep and narrow, so I can easily jump across. I land well in control on the far bank.

I'm suddenly stopped dead in my tracks by something lying on top of a raised bank of snow directly in front of me. It's a single black object in a great expanse of white. I fantasize about it being some other climbing party's discarded food parcel. Dumping surplus food and equipment to lighten the load isn't at all unusual. And if they don't need it, I do. A decent meal to eat at last. But I only manage to take another ten steps down the glacier before I'm brought to a knee-jarring stop, paralyzed with an awful fear. This black object on top of a raised bank of snow is no food parcel, it's the long black snout of a grizzly bear. Surely it can't be Scar Face? But I can clearly see the jagged scar cutting down through its nose now. How on earth did it manage to escape from the lake surrounded by nine-metre-high walls of ice? But the question becomes somewhat academic when faced with the awful reality of the bear confronting me, its eyes boring into me. I'm sure it is playing a game with me. It's the kind of game that a hunter might play with his quarry when he knows that there's not the slightest chance of his victim ever escaping.

"I'll jump inside the nearest crevasse! Do you hear that? No bear will ever get the satisfaction of killing me!" I scream across at Scar Face. "Fuck you! Bastard!" That's what I'll do. I'll simply take my chances inside the nearest crevasse. If I get injured jumping in, too bad. Anything is better than being eaten alive by a bear.

I begin to run back up the glacier, my rope, still tied

into the back of my waist belt to relieve the weight on my shoulders, trailing behind me.

I can only hope that it doesn't get caught between any of the rocks on the way. Ten steps to go! The bear is fast behind me now. I can almost feel it breathing down my neck! Just a few more steps to go . . . The jaws of the narrow crevasse loom in front of me. The ice shakes as the bear comes bounding up behind me. But it won't get me now. There's no hesitation. I jump inside the crevasse.

I come to a sudden stop, spinning around on the end of my rope. One of the knots must have caught on the lip of the crevasse. Has a single knot saved me, jammed inside the crack that the rope itself must have created as it sawed through the lip of the crevasse? Who knows the answer to that question? I'm only glad that I'm still alive.

I still can't quite see where my rope has jammed, and in trying to peer upwards at the thin strip of white light high above I start spinning around on the end of my rope again. I quickly reach out with my hands. I'm fortunate that I can touch both walls of the crevasse at the same time. I stop myself from turning.

The bear knows where I am. It towers over me now, with its huge rear legs on either side of the crevasse, looking for all the world like some monster from a bygone age. I can't help but wonder what it is going to do next. I am not kept long in suspense. With a vicious deep-throated growl it reaches deep inside the crevasse with its long forelegs, trying to hook me out. But I'm far too deep down to be within its reach. When it works this out and gives up trying to hook me out, it prowls back and forth across the top of the crevasse. Large pieces of ice, dislodged by its paws, begin to fall down on me. Whether or not this is a deliberate act by Scar Face, I don't know. But it keeps roaring down at me each time it steps over the top of the crevasse and each time it does this more large pieces of ice fall down in my direction. I try my best to dodge the heaviest lumps but this starts my rope oscillating wildly.

The bear spots this movement and begins pounding on the walls of the crevasse above me in a fury of pent up anger and frustration at not being able to reach me. My rope begins to oscillate even more wildly and it's not long before the bear is attracted to this movement. It reaches down to grasp my rope in its two huge hairy paws. The bear has it firmly in its grasp now. I've got to act decisively if I'm to save myself from being pulled out of the crevasse. I quickly stab the pick of my ice-axe deep into the wall of ice in front of me. At least I can offer some resistance now if the bear tries to pull me out but what chance do I have in a tug-of-war with a grizzly? It is already pulling quite strongly on my rope which comes tight at my waist. Then the bear begins to lift me slowly up the wall of the crevasse.

Suddenly my rope comes free of the bear's claws. I fall past my ice-axe. My full weight hits the end of my rope with a tremendous force. My ice-axe pulls out of the wall of the crevasse. I fall even further down inside the crevasse, landing on a small crumbling ledge of snow. I instinctively stab the pick of my ice-axe back into the wall. The snow collapses beneath me. I'm left jammed tightly in between the two enormous walls of ice once more, with my rope falling smoothly around my head and shoulders. But my complete rope has come down now. I'm not secured from above any more but the bear can't reach me now. However, only the pick of my ice-axe placed into the wall of the crevasse in front of me and the straps and buckles of my rucksack, digging hard into the ice behind me, are preventing me from falling further into the depths.

I've only got my ice-axe left to hold onto. But it's no use. The ice is proving to be far too brittle in this section of the crevasse for it to stay in place for very long. I'm bound to fall further down sooner or later, unless I can jam myself tight. But I still can't exert enough pressure to prevent myself from slowly sliding down. There's no substitute for a sharp pair of crampons here. Unfortunately my snowshoes are still strapped onto my boots. I continue to slide down inside the crevasse, slowly at first, then faster, in a screaming-screech of rucksack straps and buckles scraping along the ice behind me. I've got to increase the pressure on the pick of my ice-axe. But it's no use, it continues to cut a neat useless groove down through the ice in front of my face. I'm brought to a temporary stop as it strikes a rock embedded in the wall of the crevasse. But relief is short-lived as my ice-axe suddenly pulls out of the wall, taking the small rock with it, and I instantly plunge down into the darkness, with the noise of the clattering rock echoing loudly in my ears.

I come to a bone-shattering stop some eight metres down inside the crevasse, landing on my snowshoes which are still tied onto my boots. My snowshoes are side by side now, jammed tightly between the two walls of the crevasse. My knees come up to hit my chest hard. I fight to regain my breath. I can hardly breathe at all now. But I'm still in a position to realize, even in my shocked and battered state, that my snowshoes have most probably saved my life. They have formed a very effective bridge between the two walls of the crevasse, with the front ends embedded deep in the wall of ice facing me, and the back edges wedged even tighter in the wall behind me. At least I've got something to sit down on now. I'll never complain about having to carry heavy and cumbersome snowshoes again. John lent me this pair back in Anchorage. Where on earth he got such an old pair from I don't know. All I know for certain is that I'll take them back to Anchorage with me if it's the last thing that I do. That's the very least I can do for John if they save me from a slow death in the bottom of the crevasse.

But I can't remain kneeling on top of my snowshoe bridge forever. I'm going to need my crampons strapped onto my boots if I'm ever going to climb out of here. The bear continues to observe me. It seems fascinated by every move I make. It watches me put my crampons back on. Our stalemate continues and I begin to grow very cold on my snowshoe perch. But there's nothing that I can do about the cold. There's nothing that I can do about the bear either. All I can do is wait for it to go away. Bears don't have a monopoly on patience.

What I need are some warming up exercises. The trouble is that there's hardly enough room in this part of the crevasse to turn around in, let alone do any exercises. However I notice that it does become wider further along in the direction of a large snow plug. I can't see the bear now. I'm tempted to climb out. The bear might have gone away. Bears have to eat sometime. Then I think, on balance, it would be better if I stayed down here a little while longer. I begin to feel a bit warmer now with my arms wrapped tightly around my knees, lying back against my padded nylon rucksack on my snowshoe bridge. I feel sure that I can wait here for as long as it takes.

Unfortunately, the bear soon returns. I didn't think it would stay away for very long. But what on earth is it doing now? The bear is actually pissing on me! I can't believe it! The bear is urinating into the crevasse directly above me. This can't be happening? That dirty stinking bear! The bright yellow piss showers down all around me. I try to shelter beneath my cagoule. I've got to cover my nose. Bear piss stinks like hell. I watch it fizz each time it strikes the icy cold walls of the crevasse. The ice looks like it's on fire. Is the bear trying to show its utter contempt for me? Or is it trying to mark me with an extra strong scent to give a clear message to any other creatures in the area that I'm spoken for? Well,

I've got news for you bastard, I'm not spoken for! I don't belong to anyone!

My usual good humour has somehow deserted me.

Perhaps the bear thinks that the smell will drive me out of the crevasse? But it will have to think again. This is my crevasse. I'm staying here for as long as it takes for the bear to go away. It may be smelly down here. But at least I'm safe. I wonder what people back home would think of a bear pissing on someone? I bet they've never heard of that one before. But home seems a long way off now: somewhere across the vast empty wilderness, somewhere across the other side of the world. The sleep of exhaustion on the other hand is a lot closer.

I feel momentarily confused by my surroundings. I can see that I'm deep inside a crevasse. But which expedition is this one? And which glacier am I on? I must somehow piece together the events of the last few days. What on earth has been happening to me. Very slowly and gradually the awful reality of my situation dawns on me.

I still feel stiff and sore from sitting in the same cramped position on top of my snowshoes all night. The one good thing is that, amazingly, I've had a good night's sleep. But I ache all over. My legs in particular seem to have been stretched to new lengths by the weight of my heavy climbing boots, left on during the night to keep my feet warm. It's clear to me now that I've got to make a move while I'm still in a position to do so. Whether I ache all over now or not doesn't come into this equation. A thin layer of ice has already begun to form on the outer layers of my clothing. This ice adds an even greater emphasis to my thoughts. But where on earth can I possibly go inside my crevasse to get warm? Any move that I make now is obviously fraught with danger and the only place I can realistically move to is the great wedge of snow blocking the crevasse to my right. I can always run up and down on top of the snow plug. But herein lies the real danger. The crevasse becomes wider in the area of this huge snow plug, and this is bound to increase the possibility that the bear may be able to get inside. I'll just have to take a chance here. If I don't make a move soon I'm simply going to freeze. The need to take some warming up exercises and make a warm drink is proving to be a far greater incentive than my fear of the bear. I can always turn around and run back inside the narrowest part of the crevasse if it does come down.

I reach the relative safety of the snow plug after bridging across between the two walls of the crevasse, and feel a great sense of relief at having something solid beneath my feet at last. I must get some exercise now as a first priority. I begin to run up and down the snow plug, some thirty paces out and back. At least I'm starting to get warm again, and thirsty. It's not long before I have my gas stove burning red hot beneath my pan full of ice, to provide me with a large amount of warm drinking water.

There's still no sign of the bear. But I'm beginning to feel a lot warmer. The final drops of water pour down my throat. I even begin to feel quite optimistic about the future. Perhaps the bear has gone off in search of easier prey? If it has gone away this could be the opportunity I've been waiting for. It does seem to be very quiet above. The only way that I'm going to find out is if I go up and look for myself.

I start to front-point my way up the wall of the crevasse. I must move fast if I'm not to become too tired and fall off. The faint strip of light at the top of the crevasse gradually turns into a blaze of brilliant white sunlight. I place an ice-screw into the wall just a short distance below the surface of the glacier. Then I clip a short tape ladder into the eye of the ice-screw. I step very carefully up each rung of the ladder in turn. I can only hope that the ice-screw doesn't squeak when my full weight finally comes onto the top rung. But it makes no sound. I raise myself higher, then peep out over the glacier. There's still no sign of the bear though there are plenty of huge paw prints in the snow. My heart pounds in my chest as I look all around me once more. I'd like to think that I'm fully in control of this situation but I'm not.

I've got to lure Scar Face over into some kind of trap. I can't possibly continue with my journey down the glacier until I've taken care of the bear. But what kind of trap would be able to contain such a monstrous creature? I know full well that if I try to run for it the bear will soon catch me up. Any plan that I formulate now is obviously fraught with danger. The best idea I can come up with is to try and lure the bear over into an unstable area of depression I remember passing on the way up, and hope that the bear following me, being far heavier than I am, will break through into a crevasse before I do. I can think of no better plan of action.

I push down with both my hands, mantelshelfing over the well defined edge of the crevasse into daylight in all its complexity. However the moment I pull my snow-goggles down over my eyes everything comes back into focus. I must untie the rope from the front of my sit-harness. I'm never going to be able to run flat out across the glacier dragging it behind me. Why on earth do I have to tie the knots in my rope so tight? I must hurry up. I must be in full view of the bear. I push and pull on the knot in a desperate attempt to spring it loose. But I can clearly see the bear now! Scar Face is only a short distance away from me on the other side of the crevasse.

The bear has definitely seen me! I quickly spin around. The hot stinking breath of the bear suddenly envelops me. It's the most disgusting smell imaginable. The bear lunges forward towards me, catching me a glancing blow on the side of my climbing helmet, as I jump back inside the crevasse. My rope slips from my fingers, but I'm fortunate in that I fall cleanly through space without hitting the sides and my rope suddenly comes tight at my waist. I'm left hanging upside down from my top runner just a few metres above the snow plug, with the biggest headache imaginable. How on earth did the bear get behind me so fast? It continues to watch me from high above me out on the surface of the glacier. But I'm far too stiff and sore in my head, neck and shoulders to give a damn what it is going to do next.

I remain sitting on the snow plug for some time. I still feel dizzy. The bear has definitely caught me a glancing blow on the side of my climbing helmet. But I must remain conscious at all costs. There's no telling what the bear might do next.

A deathly silence continues to hang over the area of the crevasse. I could sit here forever listening to the silence. But the sound of water pouring over the sides of my cooking pan suddenly spurs me into action. It is full to the brim. How could I have forgotten that I'd left it beneath an icicle to fill up with water? I find I have an enormous thirst. I'll drink till I drown, after warming it up on my gas stove. As I drain the last drops I close my eyes in ecstasy. What a fabulous drink of water this has been. I'll collect some more from beneath another long icicle and have another huge drink later on.

But the bear is inside the crevasse! I can't believe it! Scar Face has somehow managed to gain the far side of the snow plug. I've got to get back inside the narrowest part of the crevasse before it reaches me. I drop my pan in my haste to escape. It lands on top of my gas stove I kick them both over, snatch up my stove – can't survive without that – and hook one of the prongs of the burner through a hole in the aluminium deadman belay plate on the side of my waist-belt. There's a sizzling noise as the hot metal contacts the webbing. But there's no time to stop to deal with that as I scramble along. I don't get very far. I'm brought to a sudden stop by my rope coming tight at my waist. It is still tied into the ice-screw at the top of the crevasse. I find myself being pulled slowly backwards into the snow. I'm never going to make it back to my snowshoe bridge now.

The bear, seeing me in difficulties, makes towards me faster. I'm sure it is about to throw itself at me. I cut the rope at my waist with one decisive blow of my ice-axe, and run back down the full length of the crevasse with the bear almost breathing down my neck. It must surely be within striking distance of me now. The bear lets out a terrible high-pitched scream as it prepares to sink its fangs into the back of my neck. I've had it! I'm never going to make it back into the narrowest part of the crevasse alive. My snowshoe bridge is so close. I can almost see it from here. However it's already too late to reach the safety of the narrowest part of the crevasse. I turn around to face the bear. I'll stab the pick of my ice-axe into its chest. This is going to be a last defiant gesture.

But the bear has stopped running towards me. It has stood on my hot cooking pan and forgotten all about me. All I can hear is my cooking pan being stomped into the ground.

I reach the safety of my snowshoe bridge still jammed between the two enormous walls of the crevasse, test it is still secure, and sit down to take stock in a state of near collapse. The bear is still pounding my cooking pan into the snow plug. That's one pan that's never going to be used to melt snow into water again. There are going to be some thirsty times ahead for me if I get out of here alive. My chest still heaves like hell. At least I'm safe inside the narrowest part of the crevasse. But the bear has got me trapped again now. All I can do is sit here and wait.

The bear remains crouched at the end of the snow plug just metres away. We continue to observe each other. Scar Face must hate me for what I've done. All I know is that I feel so afraid. Even the glacier seems to be holding its breath. Could this be the proverbial calm before the storm? *Please go away! Great bear!* I feel so helpless when faced with such a powerful creature. After taking care of my cooking pan the bear seems intent on taking care of me.

It begins to pound its two massive front paws into the snow close to the edge of the snow plug. I look on in horror as it repeats its actions. I can only hope that the snow plug will collapse under its blows. But it remains firm. The bear is working itself up into a fury. It stops moving, and I can see it is actually foaming at the mouth. Vile green saliva dribbles over its jaws. It must be utterly mad now, driven crazy by the hatred that it feels for me. The look on its face has only one meaning that I must be wiped off the face of the earth!

My axes are already hooked into the walls of the crevasse, one on either side of me. Their downward sloping picks should be sufficient to hold me in place on top of my snowshoe bridge should the bear decide to charge. The bear continues to wait. I continue to hold my breath.

Then suddenly, without any warning at all, the bear charges forward towards me, tearing into the narrowest part of the crevasse with its claws, hooked into the walls of ice on either side, acting as effectively as any crampons I have ever seen. The shoulders of the great bear strike the walls of the crevasse just where they begin to converge. The force of the impact is enormous. A huge shock wave is sent racing down the full length of the crevasse. My snowshoe bridge begins to shake. I shake. Then some large pieces of ice begin to fall down from somewhere high above me near the top of the crevasse. The bear gets the full force of all this snow and ice upon its head and shoulders. But it simply shrugs this debris off as if it were of no consequence at all. It continues to squeeze forward towards me until it can advance no more.

The bear is now jammed tightly in between the two converging walls of the crevasse just a short distance in front of me. It begins to heave and strain with all the strength and determination at its disposal, trying to force the two walls of the crevasse apart. Surely the bear is never going to be able to succeed? But I begin to have doubts about the end result of this great trial of strength. All I know for sure is that if it does manage to squeeze any further forward towards me, even by a small amount, I can't retreat any further back inside the crevasse. The section behind me is too narrow to admit anything. The bear's eyes begin to bulge with the effort of trying to force the two walls of the crevasse apart. I still can't believe that it will be able to squeeze any further forward towards me.

You'll never reach me inside here! Bastard!

My snowshoe bridge begins to slip very slowly further down inside the crevasse. I move down with it. *Jesus Christ!* The two walls of the crevasse are moving apart! This movement is not very much, perhaps a few centimetres at the most, but my snowshoe bridge is definitely slipping further down inside the crevasse.

I know what I must do next. I need to find my matches. (I'm sure I left a box inside one of the pockets on the outside of my rucksack.)

I've no wish to harm you great bear! Just leave me alone!

I back off to the very edge of my snowshoe bridge. I can't possibly move any further back now. The bear doesn't wait for a single moment. It suddenly reaches out with its long forelegs, claws at the ready, in a frenzied attempt to hook me off the top of my platform. Surely it will get its claws into my clothing at any moment now? I watch helplessly as the bear begins to squeeze even further forward towards me. This is the most amazing show of strength I have ever seen. I would never have believed that it could have got so close. There must be a look of absolute horror on my face now. The eyes of the bear continue to burn into me.

I pull my ice-axe out of the wall of the crevasse and stab at the bear's hairy forelegs in a desperate attempt to keep it at bay. But the pick of my ice-axe isn't long enough to have any real effect. The thick mat of hairs acts like a spongy armour plating to absorb my blows. I finally give up trying to fend it off with my ice-axe. I let go of my ice-hammer, still hooked into the wall of the crevasse beside me. I need both my hands free. But I won't be beaten here. I reach down for my gas stove, still hooked into a hole in the deadman plate on my waist-belt.

I'm truly sorry great bear! I've got no choice in the matter of what I must do next!

I slowly unscrew the burner on top of the gas cylinder. The liquid propane gas begins to squirt upwards out of the hole in the top of the cylinder the moment I expose it. It's now or never! I strike the match. The bear instinctively pulls back at the first sniff of this explosive mixture. But its reactions are too slow to save it. The mixture ignites. I hurl my gas stove like a flame-thrower into the face of the screaming bear. Its entire upper body is instantly enveloped in a red hot flaming fireball.

The heat is intense. But my head is already turned away. I cover my face with my arms. My eyes are closed. But I don't need to see anything to know what is happening to the bear. A long wailing sound follows in its wake as it runs back down the full length of the crevasse. I turn around to look the moment the heat from my exploding gas cylinder dies down. The bear is still clawing at its face. The metal prongs on top of my gas stove have somehow caught on its claws with the flames still licking up the full length of its left foreleg.

It's a terrible sight to behold. The bear gradually retreats from view.

Water continues to run down the walls of the crevasse, melted by the heat of the explosion. I take a drink of water from an icicle close to hand. I think that I'll always hate myself for what I've just done. But I had no choice in the matter.

Chapter 11

Final Reckoning

There is still no sign of the bear.

I'll never have a better chance of escaping from here. I must climb out of the crevasse now, while the bear is still occupied with its burns and trying to remove my gas stove from its claws. Then I must put my earlier plan into action. I have got to get rid of the bear. I must try to lure it to its death.

I'm left gasping for breath after front-pointing my way up the wall of the crevasse in one long pitch. I haven't a moment to lose. The bear could return at any moment, and once I stand upright on the surface of the glacier there's no hiding place. What I have to do is take advantage of some nearby dodgy ground I noticed on my way up. It forms a crater-like depression which probably held a lake at some time in the past. The floor must be riddled with crevasses to drain the water. In the centre there's a tower of ice. If I can get to that tower without going through the surface myself, I can climb it, lure the bear into the crater after me and wait for its body weight to do the rest.

I hesitate over jumping into the huge crater. But I don't really have any choice in the matter of what I must do next. I jump down onto the floor of the depression. My heart pounds in my chest. Whatever I do I mustn't lose my nerve here. I arrive at the base of the tower sweating with fear. I'm sure the ice moved beneath me on several occasions as I ran across the floor of the depression. But I must climb up on top of the tower now before the bear comes back. I literally throw myself up at the wall of ice, front-pointing my way up towards the top. I glance behind me. There's still no sign of the bear.

The top of the tower is as flat as a billiard table and not much larger. I lie back in the snow and close my eyes for a moment. I must rest before I do anything else. I ache all over now. Where has Scar Face got to? It definitely isn't inside the moat-like depression surrounding me. At least I'm safe up here on top of the tower. I sit down on top of my rucksack to wait.

What a marvellous view I've got of every feature on the surface of the glacier from up here. I can see for several kilometres in all directions. If only the sun would appear. Unfortunately there's nothing but a thin blanket of grey cloud drifting past low over my head. No sun, no chance of a decent meal to warm me either. I've only got three small pieces of white candle wax left to eat. They are meant to last me for three days, half a candle per day.

There's no reason why I shouldn't eat today's ration now. The small piece of wax tastes wonderful in my mouth. Now I've only got two pieces left to eat. All I can do is dream about food perched on my rucksack on top of my pillar. My right hand is moving. It reaches inside my trouser pocket. I can't seem to stop my hand from lifting the two remaining small pieces of candle wax out of my pocket. But if I eat them now I'll have nothing left. I squeeze the two pieces together in one wedge. I seem mesmerized by the sight of food. I mustn't eat tomorrow's candle wax! *For God's sake don't do it, David!* I begin to plead with myself. *Please don't eat it!* But my right hand refuses to obey and places the wax in my mouth. Any claim I've had to strong willpower simply evaporates. I bite hard into the soft white candle wax. It seems to taste of anything that I've ever dreamed of eating. But my willpower has been broken. Two small pieces of white candle wax have managed to do to me what nothing has ever succeeded in doing before. The effect on my morale is shattering.

Self-discipline is what I have always prided myself on. It has helped me not to give up in tight corners in the Alps as well as Alaska. It has helped save other lives than mine. I have never given up the struggle before. My survival to this day has all been the result of discipline! The ultimate test is here and now! If I swallow this candle wax, I tell myself, I will be finished! I will simply die out here! Perhaps I've waited all my life to be tested in this way. The candle wax is still in my mouth. I have a clear choice. I can simply eat it now and choose to die out here in the mountains. Or I can spit it out of my mouth and choose to live.

I watch mesmerized as the sweet-tasting candle wax falls straight down the side of the tower. Tears form in my eyes now. I'm crying because I've got nothing left to eat. There are tears in my eyes also for a smouldering grizzly bear. But they are a small price to pay for the return of my willpower. I was once told that wherever the mind goes, the body follows. In spitting the candle wax out of my mouth I have decided to go all the way to Anchorage and beyond.

I can see the bear now and it is definitely coming towards me. All I've got to do is blow my whistle in order to attract it over into the moat. But I'm still far too afraid to blow it. I'm still fearful what the bear may do next. My whistle remains frozen in between my lips. No sound comes out of the end.

The bear continues to lumber forward towards me. Then it comes up against the edge of the crevasse that was the scene of our last encounter. The bear stops just once to sniff the air, as it pads along the rim, and to run a huge paw in a cat-like way over its burnt face. It is still too far away from me for me to see the real extent of its injuries. Then it begins to roll over and over in the snow. It must be trying to get some relief from the burns inflicted by my flaming gas cylinder. I can see the damage to the bear's upper body now. It doesn't look to be too severe. Its thick shaggy coat has obviously saved it from far worse injuries. I'm glad in a way, part of me has never wanted to harm it and still recoils at having to do so.

The bear remains lying down in the snow for some time, still unaware of my presence on top of the tower. I must somehow entice it over into my trap, but I still can't pluck up the courage to blow my whistle. Then the bear stretches and continues to prowl forward along the edge of the crevasse, getting closer to me all the time, stopping occasionally to look down into the darkness within the crevasse itself, staring intently down into the icy cold depths below, sniffing the air, looking for me.

The bear still hasn't noticed me on top of the tower. I'm still the silent observer trying to plot its downfall. I'm going to have to use myself as live bait in order to lure it over into the unstable area of the crater. I can only hope that it breaks through into a crevasse quickly, because if it does get across the floor of the depression unscathed, it might, I now realize, just be able to reach up to the top of the tower. But that thought is too awful to contemplate. I must act now before I lose my nerve here completely. I raise my plastic whistle to my lips. I take a long deep breath. But no sound comes out of the end.

At this point the bear comes across my trail in the snow, leading away from the edge of the crevasse in the direction of the depression. Its coat literally begins to bristle. Then the bear lets out a tremendous roar. Scar Face sniffs the air once more before bounding off along my trail towards me until it finally spots me on top of the tower and stops dead in its tracks on the very edge of the moat-like depression to stare up at me.

I can clearly see the bear's face now. It has been completely distorted by the fierce heat of my exploding gas cylinder. Small puffs of smoke can still be seen coming out from beneath the bear's smouldering bodily hair to shroud its melted facial features. It's a terrible sight. The bear has not been mortally injured, but it has been even more disfigured. There's nothing more that I can do now but wait.

The bear begins to prowl up and down the far edge of the moat and I, needing to do something to ease the tension, begin to walk around the top of my tower. Before I know it I find we are tracking each other, each prowling round in perfect circles, with me walking a small one on my tower and the bear having to cover a far larger distance around the edge of the crater – and yet still striving to keep up with me. The bear is very determined in its efforts. We remain locked together, with only the width of the moat separating us, until I start to slow down. The bear starts to slow down also. So it is definitely trying to compete with me. As if mesmerized by this horrific game we are playing, I break into a run, just for the hell of it. The bear is having to move extremely fast now in order to keep up with me.

The bear is definitely trying to race me. But if there is a race, there has to be a winner, and I hold the initiative in this race. Whoever holds the initiative in any race usually wins. "You're never going to be able to keep up with me now, bastard!" I shout across at the bear as I run even faster, with the bear having to take great bounding leaps in order to keep up. But this bizarre race can't go on for ever. As if acknowledging the fact, the bear brakes to a furious halt, screaming at me with its two huge front paws slamming into the ice on the edge of the depression. It seems to be going absolutely crazy now. It backs off and charges back to the edge of the moat. Though it can't possibly jump the gap separating us, I take several quick steps backwards, almost falling off the top of the tower in my fright. I never expected it to move so fast. It's a good job that this charge was only a bluff.

This is one game that is definitely over.

I'm left with a terrible feeling that all hell is about to break loose. I must put my plan into action before I lose my nerve completely. I begin to taunt the bear. I sit on top of my rucksack with my legs dangling down over the edge of the huge block of ice. "Come on, bastard! Get my legs if you dare!" The bear continues to prowl up and down the edge of the depression, completely ignoring me now. It must be able to see my legs dangling down so invitingly. "Come on, bastard! Do something!" But it still refuses to leave the relative safety of the glacier.

I've a terrible feeling that my plan is not going to work. If the bear stays where it is on the glacier, I'll be the one that's trapped on top of the tower. I think I'll have a drink of water while I'm waiting. I turn round to look for my water-bottle inside my rucksack. I'm sure that I placed it inside one of my woollen jumpers in order to stop it freezing. The moment I turn my back the bear moves. I'm sure I heard it drop down into the moat. But I mustn't turn around yet. I've got to keep my nerve here. I must give it a clear chance of falling through into a crevasse. I can still hear it moving across the floor of the depression. It must be getting close to me now. Then suddenly the bear is directly beneath me.

It hurls itself up at my legs dangling down temptingly over the side of the tower. I only just manage to lift them up in time. The bear's claws slam into the wall of ice beneath me. The tower shakes. I drop my water-bottle in sheer fright. The bear falls backwards into the depression. But it hasn't fallen through into a crevasse. My plan to trap it is clearly not going to work. The bear slowly regains its feet. But where has it got to? I throw myself flat on top of the tower. Scar Face is nowhere to be seen. I drive the pick of my ice-axe deep into the ice on top of the tower. I don't want to be thrown off when it makes its next move. But I must find out which side the bear is trying to climb up. I must be ready for it when it appears over the top of the tower. I grasp the head of my ice-axe even tighter now. I hardly dare look down into the depression. But I've got to do that if I'm to find out which wall of the tower the bear is trying to climb up. It is definitely not beneath this one. But there are three others. I crawl slowly across towards the opposite side of the tower after changing hands on the head of my ice-axe. The bear's not beneath this one either. It could even be moving around in order to confuse me.

The bear's claws suddenly appear over the edge directly in front of my face. I immediately stab the pick of my ice-axe into one of its paws. It lets out a scream and falls backwards into the depression, fortunately not taking my ice-axe with it. I must see where it has landed before it has a chance to recover. But the bear is far too quick for me. It is already on its feet and immediately throws itself up at the same wall. There's a tremendous crash as it strikes the iron hard ice. The tower shakes once more. My water-bottle slides off the top of the tower. But I'm already braced lying down and far too slow to save it. I'm left hanging onto the pick of my ice-axe as if my very life depended upon it.

My legs begin to swing over to one side of the tower as it starts to lean over at an alarming angle to the wall of ice surrounding the depression. I pull myself back towards the centre of the top of the tower, using the picks on both my axes. There's another loud crash as the bear strikes the tower and its huge hairy paws suddenly reappear. My heart pounds in my chest as I bring the pick of my ice-hammer slicing down into one of the bear's forelegs this time. It screams out loud. Blood spurts everywhere. Then it falls backwards off the side of the tower with another reverberating crash. My ice-hammer is torn from my grasp, caught up in the thick mat of blood-stained hairs on the bear's left leg. It flies across the full width of the moat, landing somewhere on the glacier. That's done it now! I'm going to need my ice-hammer if I'm ever going to climb out of here. I grasp my ice-axe even tighter. If I lose them both

I'm never going to be able to escape from here. I could find myself trapped inside the depression forever.

The tower is clearly moving beneath me. The bear is trying to push it over. It roars up at me, a terrible high pitched scream as it pushes against the side of the tower, causing it to rock ever so gently back and forth. I dig the front-points on my crampons deeper into the ice. I must stop my legs from swinging over the edge of the tower. But the huge block of ice suddenly stops moving. It is left tilted over at a frightening angle. Why has the bear stopped pushing? It suddenly goes very quiet. But not for long. The bear suddenly starts to pound on the side of the tower with its two massive front paws. The vibrations pass up the full length of the huge block of ice until I can feel each individual one in my knees and forearms which are pressed hard into the ice. There are some terrible noises coming from deep within the base of the huge block of ice now. It groans and starts to lean over even further. I begin to realize that it's only a matter of time before I'm tipped off the top. There's nothing that I can do about it other than to hang on to the head of my ice-axe and hope for a miracle to occur.

The bear goes quiet once more. What is it up to now? Then I hear a very definite droning coming from somewhere lower down on the glacier. The bear must be listening to this same noise. The droning becomes louder. Then louder and louder still. The complete valley floor is filled with the noise of an aircraft coming directly up the glacier towards me. I can see it approaching the top of a barrier of séracs lower down on the glacier now. It has got to pass directly overhead. I must signal to the pilot. I begin to wave my rucksack, holding it in my one free hand. I still daren't let go of my ice-axe. I'm sure that the pilot will land on the glacier if he sees I am in trouble. He can then shoot the bear. He is bound to have a rifle with him as part of his standard survival kit. So I continue to wave like hell, as the aircraft approaches me through a small gap in the clouds, wings glistening in the bright sunlight. There's the distinct possibility that John could be the pilot. He could be looking for me now. "I'm over here, John!" I begin to shout futiley up at the aircraft.

The aircraft passes directly over the top of my head and enters the clouds once more. The pilot has obviously had to gain altitude in order to clear the summit of Mount Deborah at the head of the glacier. I doubt he will be coming back in my direction today. The noise from the aircraft gradually fades into oblivion, and I return to guessing from which direction I am next going to be attacked by the bear.

The bear starts to pound on the side of the tower once more and large cracks begin to appear in each of the four corners, then radiate towards me. The tower is definitely starting to fall to pieces. The top of the huge block of ice is no longer the safe haven that it once was. I've simply got to take my chances in the depression. I'll jump down at the first opportunity and run for it. But there's no point in kidding myself either. I know full well that I'm never going to be able to outrun the bear.

As the tower begins to tilt over even further, there's hardly any time left to put my plan into action. I'm left hanging from the shaft of my ice-axe with my legs dangling very close to the ground. I must climb up onto the highest corner of the tower before the bear gets its claws into my legs. Scar Face is already directly beneath me. I fancy there's a horrendous expression of triumph on its snarling face as it reaches up for my legs. But the bear misses them at its first attempt. I lift them higher up towards my chest now. Scar Face doesn't hesitate for a single moment before leaping high into the air once more. This time the bear hooks its claws into the edge of the tower close to my legs. I've got to stab the pick of my ice-axe into its skull the moment it appears on top of the tower. I'll use the pick like a knife. I'm never going to get another opportunity to kill the bear. This is my only chance of staying alive.

The bear lets out a victorious roar as it pulls up over the side of the tower to confront me. I raise the pick of my ice-axe high above my head. But the weight of the bear is already proving to be too much for the tower, leaning over as it already is in the most dramatic manner possible. I have to let go of my ice-axe to grasp the edge of the tower with both my hands as it slowly begins to topple over, landing on top of the screaming bear. Scar Face must surely be crushed beneath the tower now. I slide slowly backwards, down the sloping side of the tower, landing safely in the snow, next to my water-bottle. There's a long hideous wail coming from the bear. The ground begins to shake. Then the main bulk of the tower itself begins to tremble. I hardly dare open my eyes as I shelter beneath one of its toppled walls.

The noise of falling debris gradually subsides. There's a new equilibrium in the depression now. There's a new order around the base of the tower.

I feel an immense sense of relief with the bear at last destroyed under what must be one of the world's largest tombstones. If only I had the time to carve out an epitaph on this monstrous block of ice, I'd write the simple words, "In memory of a great bear!"

Chapter 12

Survivor

I soon climb out of the depression. There's still no sign of the bear, just a great red stain in the snow, oozing out from beneath one of the long walls of the tower. Scar Face must be well and truly dead by now. I raise my hand in genuine recognition of a formidable fighter in its final resting place.

Now I must determine the right snow slope by which to leave the glacier, the one that will lead me back up onto the ridge overlooking my food supplies down in the ravine. All the slopes bordering the glacier have a similar look when viewed from below. I tell myself I recognize one of them and take my chance.

I arrive sweating on the far bank of the bergschrund after crossing my final hair-raising snowbridge, and turn my back on the glacier that had provided me with so many hazards.

I begin to climb up the snow slope that will eventually lead me back up onto the crest of the ridge overlooking Ravine Camp 3. The foreshortened crest looks reasonably close from down here. But all my mountaineering experience warns me that there's a lot more to it than meets the eye. The effort of climbing up the snow slope is requiring a willpower to match any that I have summoned up earlier. I must reach my goal. My rest stops become more frequent.

I think I'll have another one now. I don't see why I shouldn't stop if I want to. I must rest before I drop dead in my tracks. I'm going to have to stop climbing soon in order to get my breath back anyway. I lean forward with both my forearms resting on top of my left knee, the one closest in towards the slope itself. But I must not angle my body in towards the slope proper. If I do that my feet will slip. If that happens, I will fall. If I come off on such a steep snow slope, I will surely die.

I must keep alert to the dangers surrounding me . . .

I must never forget . . .

I can hardly think at all now . . .

But my breathing gradually returns to normal. My body craves food. I long for sleep. But my determination to survive is still very strong. It's this one factor that starts me moving stubbornly uphill once more. It's a never-ending struggle against the forces of nature itself. But the slope eventually levels off, and I step up onto a beautiful ridge covered in snow. What a relief to be walking on a reasonably flat surface once more. Thank goodness that most of the uphill climbing on this expedition is over. I feel an enormous sense of relief to have put the snow slope behind me. I stride purposefully forward along the ridge now towards my food supplies buried down in the ravine.

Slender columns of ice now block my path. The way they have been scoured by the elements is as if some master craftsman had been to work up here sculpting the faces of unknown climbers into the columns. Unfortunately, I find myself being forced further away from my intended route. All these changes begin to confuse me. I'm not at all sure now which is the correct route down to the ravine camp. I could easily end up going down into the wrong valley. As if to make matters worse, it starts to snow. I can hardly see my hand in front of my face. It's becoming painfully obvious to me now that in these poor weather conditions I must give up my search for my food supplies. It's far more important for me just to lose altitude now.

I begin to climb down the first convenient snow slope to appear along the side of the ridge. The lower I descend into the valley below the worse the snow conditions become underfoot. I only just manage to stay in control of my feet, once more using my boots like skis. What fun it is to ski down the slope. What a wonderful experience! My loud shouts of glee echo back and forth off the surrounding tundra slopes. What if a bear hears me? I'm past caring now. Fuck the bears! Why shouldn't I shout as loud as I want to? Who says that I've got to tiptoe my way silently across Alaska? I'm slowly dying of starvation here. Do you hear that, world? But I've still got some rights. With no food left to eat, I'm going to be dead soon anyway. So why shouldn't I shout as loud as I want to? "Yes! Fuck the bears!" I execute another complete series of beautiful shallow stem turns. To the left of me. To the right of me. To the left once more. I've been through hell on this expedition. I'll shout as loud as I fucking well want to now!

I continue downhill, travelling over smooth snow and bare rock patches, interspersed with large areas of watery boggy ground. Some of the boulders in these islands are enormous. It's as if at some time in the past a huge explosion had taken place and showered the area with debris. These monstrous boulders make it very difficult for me to walk in a straight line in any given direction. Soon I must find somewhere safe to spend the night, while I puzzle out exactly where I am. I must stop before I fall asleep on my feet. The trouble is that I feel so terribly tired. I can only seem to walk for a few minutes at a time now before I get tired and have to stop. I might as well have another rest now. I'll simply sit down on top of this huge boulder. It's a wonderful feeling to be doing nothing. There are going to be no more long approach marches on any of my expeditions from now on. I'm going to fly in to the mountains in future. I'm not going to carry another heavy load again either. I'm going to travel as light as I possibly can. Perhaps I'll remain here with my feet dangling down over the edge of this huge boulder forever.

I've got nothing left to eat now. I don't think that I've got anything to look forward to any more. I'm not at all certain which direction I must take now to find either my food cache in the ravine or the Denali Highway. The truth is that I'm lost. So why should I bother to move in any direction at all? I close my eyes. I lie back on top of the boulder. I open my hands. My ice-axe slips from my right hand. My empty water-bottle falls out of my left hand. My ice-axe continues to swing to and fro, still attached to my wrist on the end of a short tape sling.

"You're free to go now! You can leave, ice-axe!" I find myself talking to it. I must be losing my mind. I feel dizzy. The world seems to be spinning around. But I'll talk to my ice-axe if I want to. I'll speak to the rocks if necessary.

"I won't be needing you any more, ice-axe! We've climbed our last mountain together!" More words begin to form, although none pass my lips. I'm too tired to speak. Did I really talk to my ice-axe? It's so hard to remember what happened only a few moments ago. It's as if I've used up all the remaining glucose reserves in my body. I seem to have hit a brick wall. The same one that I ran into in the Paris Marathon at mile 22 in 1974. I'm living in a slow motion world of facts now. But did I really speak to my ice-axe? I still don't know the answer to that question.

Snowflakes are falling out of the sky all around me now. They slowly begin to accumulate in the palms of my hands. These two small piles of sculptured ice reach a critical angle, then begin to trickle down through the gaps between my fingers. The air is full of them now. I can almost feel each individual snowflake as it lands on the bare sensitive skin of my hands and face, my cheeks in particular. Icy cold snowflakes, melting in my hot palms, then running down my cheeks. These tiny particles of ice slowly start to take the heat away from my hands and face. My hands in particular are beginning to freeze. These snowflakes falling out of the sky feel like tears. I'm too tired to cry. I'm too tired even to think any more. If I don't act soon I'm simply going to die out here in the wilderness. But I couldn't really care less about anything any more, or what eventually happens to me. The snow continues to build up, in many fine layers, on top of my clothing.

I'm starting to hallucinate. I'm sure that I can see angels in the snow clouds above me. I'm sure that I'm going to die soon. Then a small voice reminds me commandos don't just lie down and die. I remember my training at Lympstone in Devon and that green beret of mine that represented well over a year of the most gruelling training imaginable. But look at me now. What a pathetic specimen. Has all my training been in vain? Have none of the lessons taught me ever been learnt? I've got to stand up now or this time I will die out here in the wilderness. If I don't start moving soon I'm simply going to freeze to death on top of this rock.

I open my eyes. I take a long deep breath. I take a tight hold on the shaft of my ice-axe once more. I sit up on top of the boulder. I allow myself to slide slowly down to the ground. I land on my knees in the wet snow. I brush the snowflakes from the front of my clothing. I'm ready to fight once more. I wander off into the cold Alaskan night.

I continue walking in silence along the floor of the valley, still trying to lose as much height as possible. This is not a dark European night, I can still see where to place my feet. But is it really night-time now? The time could be somewhere in the late afternoon for all I know? Or is it early evening? All I know for sure is that soon I'm simply going to fall asleep on my feet.

But there are definitely lights ahead of me. I can see two powerful headlights moving on top of the next rise in front of me! This must surely be the Nenana River below me now. The lights must be coming from a vehicle out on the Denali Highway. I get across the river as quickly as possible and stagger up the slippery slope on the far bank into the woods, then out of the tall spruce trees and onto the highway.

It's a pick-up truck, headlights full on. I must flag it down. I need to tie some material onto the shaft of my ice-axe in order to stop the vehicle. My T-shirt is going to have to do the job. The truck jerks to a halt.

"Is that you, John?"

"David? Are you in trouble?"

John leans over and helps me into the passenger seat. He watches while I scrabble for food under the dashboard. He listens as I grow more incoherent with relief.

"It was fantastic John . . . the mountain was everything I'd ever hoped it would be, and the glacier, and the wilderness . . . and there was this bear . . ."

Glossary of
Climbing Terms

ABSEIL. A method of descending over steep rocks, snow or ice by sliding down a fixed double rope.

BASE CAMP. The principal camp, close to the foot of the mountain, from which the attempts to climb it are made.

BELAY. To tie oneself to a firm anchor point.

BERGSCHRUND. The last big crevasse across the head of a glacier.

BIVOUAC. A temporary lightweight encampment in the mountains.

CAGOULE. A long thin waterproof jacket.

CAIRN. A pile of stones erected to mark a summit, a spot height, a pass, etc. Cairns are also put up at short intervals along a mountain path to mark the way in misty weather.

CHIMNEY. A fissure in a rock face which will admit the complete body.

COL. A pass. A major gap in a ridge between two peaks. A dip in a ridge between two high points.

CONTOUR. An imaginary line on the ground drawn on a map to join up all points of equal height above sea level.

CORNICE. An overhanging lip of hardened snow raised along the crest of a ridge.

CRACK. A fissure in a rock face.

CRAMPONS. Steel spikes fixed to a frame which are strapped to the soles of climbing boots to get a purchase on snow and ice.

CREVASSE. A split in the surface of the glacier.

DEADMAN. An aluminium belay plate for use as an anchor in soft snow.

DESCENDEUR. A friction device for abseiling.

DIRETTISSIMA. A route which follows a direct line to the summit of a mountain, as opposed to a more natural one.

DUVET. Down jacket.

ETRIER. A short lightweight ladder, made from sewn tape or alloy rungs fixed to a thin cord, used to assist climbing overhanging rock or ice.

FRONT-POINTING. A technique used to climb straight up steep snow or ice by kicking the front-points of twelve-point crampons into the slope, in conjunction with an ice-axe and ice-hammer in either hand to maintain balance.

GLACIER. A river of ice.

GLISSADE. A controlled descent of a snow slope by sliding on one's boots.

ICE-SCREW. A hollow tubular metal screw with an eylet through which a rope can be passed for protection.

ICE TOOLS. An axe and a hammer for cutting steps in snow and ice. Also used for probing for crevasses, arresting falls, and as a break for glissading.

JUMAR CLAMP. A mechanical device for climbing up a fixed rope.

KARABINER. A D-shaped link made with a spring-hinged gate in one side. The main uses of karabiners are joining the climbing rope to the climber's harness; linking the rope to abseil points and for running belays, and joining etriers and rope to pitons in artificial climbing.

MANTELSHELFING. A technique used to climb up onto a narrow ledge. There are three main steps: a pull up to raise the body; a press up position with both arms; cocking one leg up onto the ledge and slowly standing up.

MORAINE. Piles of debris brought down by the movement of a glacier.

PITCH. A section of climbing between two stances.

PITON. A piece of metal designed to be hammered into a crack in a rock face, to serve as a belay, a running belay, or an artificial aid.

RUNNING BELAY. (Runner.) A belay through which the active rope runs at an intermediate point between a moving climber and a fixed one. The object of placing a runner is to reduce the potential falling distance of the leader; and to give him the confidence to make difficult moves.

SCREE. Areas of loose boulders and small stones covering a steep slope below a rock face.

SÉRAC. A tower of ice in an icefall.

SIT-HARNESS. A wide tape device, attached in to the rope, which goes around the waist and criss-crossing between the legs to provide a comfortable seat in artificial climbing. It also distributes the energy of a fall.

SNOWBRIDGE. A bridge of snow spanning a crevasse.

SNOW-GOGGLES. Tinted lenses set in aluminium frames, or spectacle frames with side hoods, designed to protect the eyes from ultra-violet rays being reflected up off the snow.

SOLO CLIMBING. Climbing alone, and for a large part of any route, climbing unroped. Solo climbing should only be practised by experienced mountaineers on climbs which they know to be well within their own limits.

SPINDRIFT. Powder snow being blown by the wind.

STEP. A sudden rise in a ridge.

TRUE RIGHT/TRUE LEFT BANK. As in the direction of flow of the glacier.

VERGLAS. A film of ice on rocks caused by running water freezing and by mist condensing and freezing on the rocks.

WIND SLAB. A snow crust, formed by wind-blown snow which settles insecurely on top of old snow. The crust is usually hard, but is unstable and tends to fracture and break off very easily.